AF225287

# CRICUT JOY

# vol. 2

## THE COMPLETE GUIDE TO MASTER YOUR CRICUT JOY MACHINE WITH SIMPLE PROJECTS

© Copyright 2020 by Sienna Tally - All rights reserved.

The following book is reproduced below to provide information that is as accurate and reliable as possible. Regardless, purchasing this book can be seen as consent because both the publisher and the author of this book are in no way experts on the topics discussed within. Any recommendations or suggestions that are made herein are for entertainment purposes only. Professionals should be consulted as needed before undertaking any of the actions endorsed herein.

This declaration is deemed fair and valid by both the American Bar Association and the Committee of Publishers Association and is legally binding throughout the United States. Furthermore, the transmission, duplication, or reproduction of any of the following work, including specific information, will be considered an illegal act irrespective of if it is done electronically or in print. This extends to creating a secondary or tertiary copy of the work or a recorded document and is only allowed to express written consent from the publisher. All additional rights reserved.

The information in the following pages is broadly considered a truthful and accurate account of facts. As such, any inattention, use, or misuse of the information in question by the reader will render any resulting actions solely under their purview. There are no scenarios in which the publisher or the original author of this work can be in any fashion deemed liable for any hardship or damages that may befall them after undertaking the information described herein.

Additionally, the following pages' information is intended only for informational purposes and should thus be thought of as universal. As befitting its nature, it is presented without assurance regarding its prolonged validity or interim quality. Trademarks that are mentioned are done without written consent and can in no way be considered an endorsement from the trademark holder.

Made with love

by

Sienna

Tally

# Table of Contents


INTRODUCTION...................................................................6

CHAPTER 1:  WHAT CAN YOU MAKE WITH CRICUT JOY........................8

-First Step...................................................................24
-Second Step................................................................24

CHAPTER 2: MAKING YOUR FIRST PROJECT IDEA..........................24

-Third Step.................................................................26
-How to Upload Images with A Cricut Joy.............................29

CHAPTER 3: HOW TO USE DESIGN SPACE IN CRICUT JOY..................30

-The Design Program.......................................................32
-The Cricut Joy Design Space...........................................32
-How to use Cricut.........................................................33
-Design Space...............................................................33
-How to Edit Images in....................................................33
-Design Space...............................................................33
-How to Upload Basic......................................................36
-Images to Design Space.................................................36
-How about Cricut Access?...............................................37
-How to Find Cricut........................................................40
-Access Resources.........................................................40
-How to Save and Share Files on Cricut Joy........................40

-Limitations........................................................................44

CHAPTER 4: BEST CRICUT JOY PROJECTS................................48

-How to make Cricut Joy labels.............................................48
-Projects ideas....................................................................52

CHAPTER 5  CRICUT JOY F.A.Q.............................................92

CONCLUSION ....................................................................104

# Introduction

First of all, thank you for purchasing my guide: "Cricut Joy vol. 2 ". I'm Sienna Tally, and in this guide, the long-awaited follow-up to "Cricut Joy Vol 1", I will take you on a journey of discovery into the colorful world of Cricut projects. Specifically, we will learn what types of objects the latest Cricut model can create, but most importantly, how to make fantastic creations for you and your family.

The Cricut is an incredible machine for individuals into adoration making and for or individuals who need to cut many things with various kinds of materials. A Cricut is a cutting machine, and fantasy worked out as expected for some crafters. Below are some advantages of having a Cricut machine.

Something that sets the Cricut Maker separated from other cutting machines is that it has a few exchangeable edges. Need to do some sewing, sewing, paper, create foam, balsa wood, felt, foil, burlap, cardstock, grain box, creased cardboard, basic food item sack, or a bazillion (alright, slight embellishment) different undertakings? This machine can deal with it to such an extent!

Set your eyes on the bigger goals. Once you have the expense of provisions, you'll be more ready to value your things to sell. Remember the time it took you to make the thing except if you like working for nothing. A dependable general guideline is your selling cost will be between two to multiple times your expense of provisions. Try not to stress over individuals snickering at you that it's excessive. You're unique, you've limited your field, and you're a specialist and the best at what you do. Besides, you're utilizing quality items (more on that soon).

Gain some new useful knowledge every day. Don't fear gaining from the individuals who have gone before you. You don't need to make sense of everything all alone. In any event, toward the beginning of your Cricut business, you'll be accomplishing more advertising than making. Make it an objective to gain some new useful knowledge consistently that relates to your business. And lastly, do quality control. Sell quality items. Quality successes over amount each day of the week

You even get 50 free ventures alongside your Cricut Maker. It incorporates sewing designs, iron-on, vinyl decals, and that's just the beginning. Do a great deal of sewing? Or then again, perhaps you wish you could do a ton of sewing? It is the machine for you. It removes the hard (and dull) portions of sewing ventures so you can get down to the pleasant part quicker.

This book will give you great advice on projects that you can do with your particular joy machine. There are some that individual devices can cut, and others can't miss very much. If you are doing heavy-duty projects, you will need a machine that can do this. This is why we have compiled the best information for you.

# Chapter 1
# What can you make with Cricut Joy

To give you some ideas to get you started on where to look, here is a list of 100 crafts you can do with your Cricut system to make your skills unique to you genuinely!

## 3D WOOD PUZZLES

These are fantastic fun, and they make such an excellent final product when put together.

## 3D FOAM PUZZLES

Foam is just as sturdy for 3D puzzles, and you can take them apart, put them back together, knock them down, and more and they bounce right back. These make such a great gift for young children.

## 3D WALL ART

Art that pops off your wall and makes a statement about who you are to all your guests is something people pay a lot of money to have. Put a little piece of your creative self on your

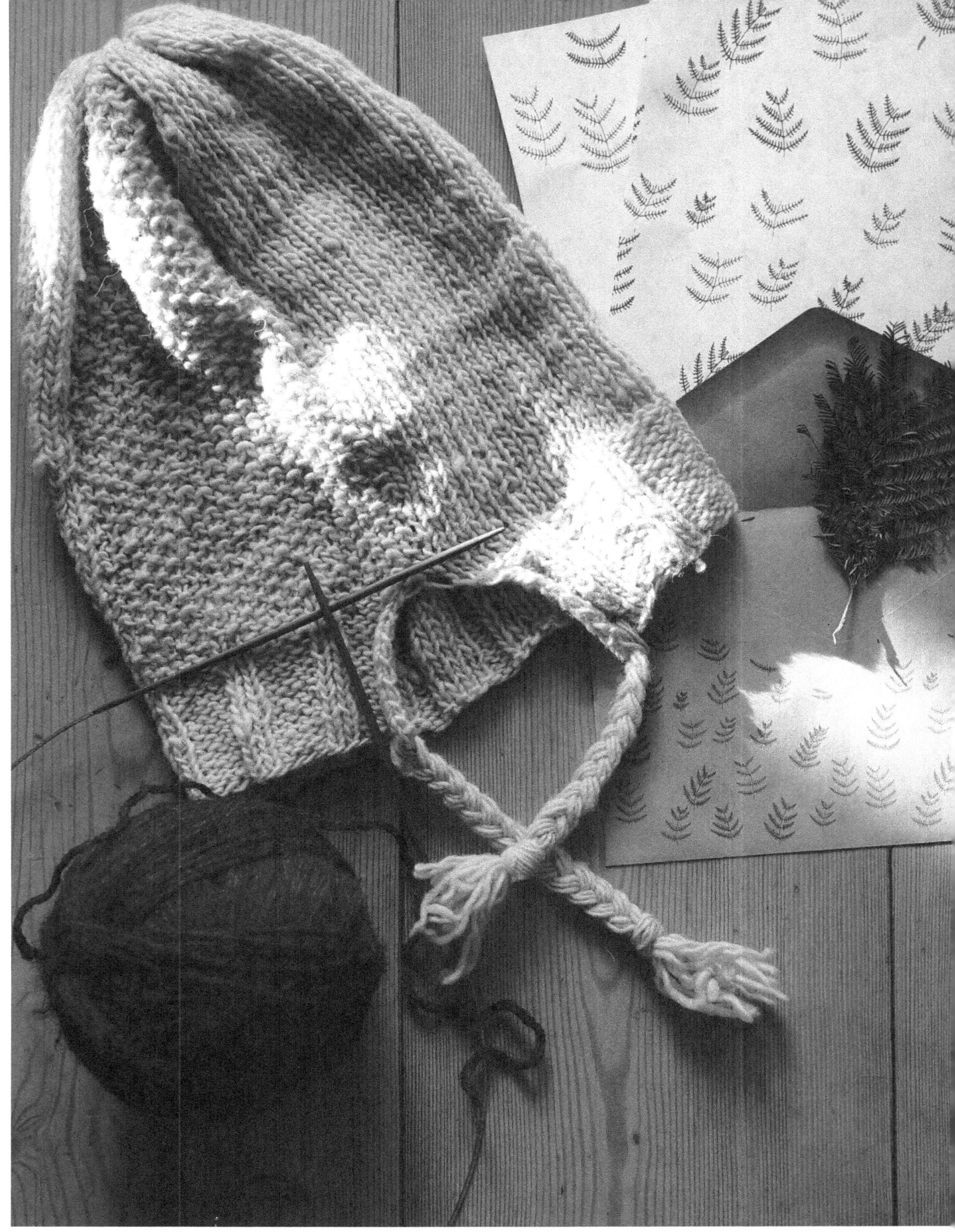

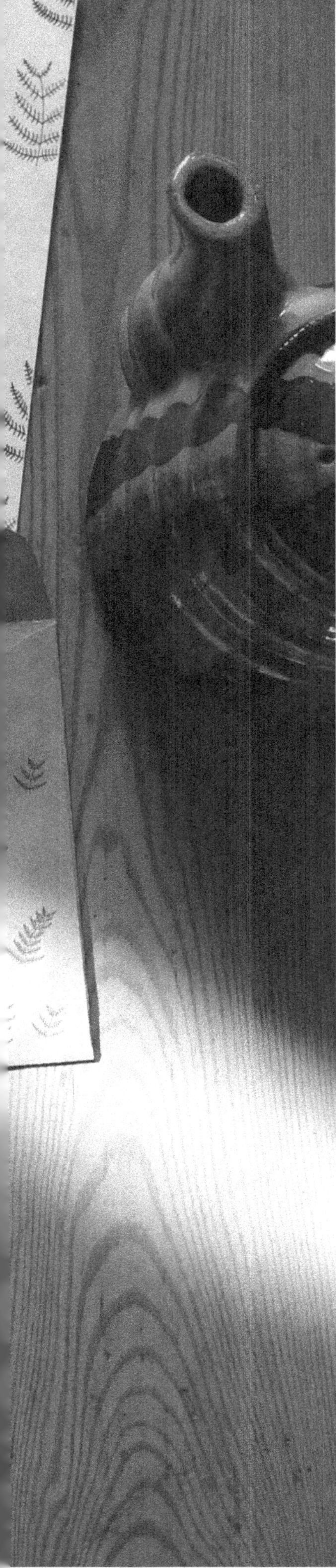

wall and show off your creativity!

# APRONS

If you have a lot of passion in the kitchen, your apron is a great way to add a personalized touch to your experience. With a character you love, a funny saying, or just a monogram, you can own the kitchen.
Banners
Any occasion is made more official with a banner! With Cricut, you can use your materials to create a banner that is unique and which will beautifully commemorate the occasion at hand.

# BEANIES

For any outdoor activity that's going to be happening during the winter months, a knit cap is a great way to keep warm. Having one with your design emblazoned on the side is sure to not only elevate the style of the hat but to make others wonder where they can get one just like it!

# BEER STEINS

The dollar store will often have blank glass beer mugs calling out to crafters to decorate them. Make a memorable gift for the beer lover in your life!

# BOOKMARKS

Bookmarks are such a simple craft, but they're almost always needed! Replace the grocery receipt in the middle of their book with something fun and personal!

# BUMPER STICKERS

Something to occupy the drivers behind you in traffic will always be in style. Make some fun statements for you and your friends to put on the bumper!

# BUSINESS CARDS

Business cards that are cut from premium stock and the shapes can be so expensive. Printing your designs on cardstock with a standard printer and cutting out dynamic systems is sure to catch the eye of potential customers.

# BUSINESS MARKETING MATERIALS

Why stop at business cards when you can make standees, door hangers, and so much more?

# CAKE TOPPERS

Got a themed birthday party coming up? Use plastic or metal to make a beautifully themed cake topper that will blow away your guests!

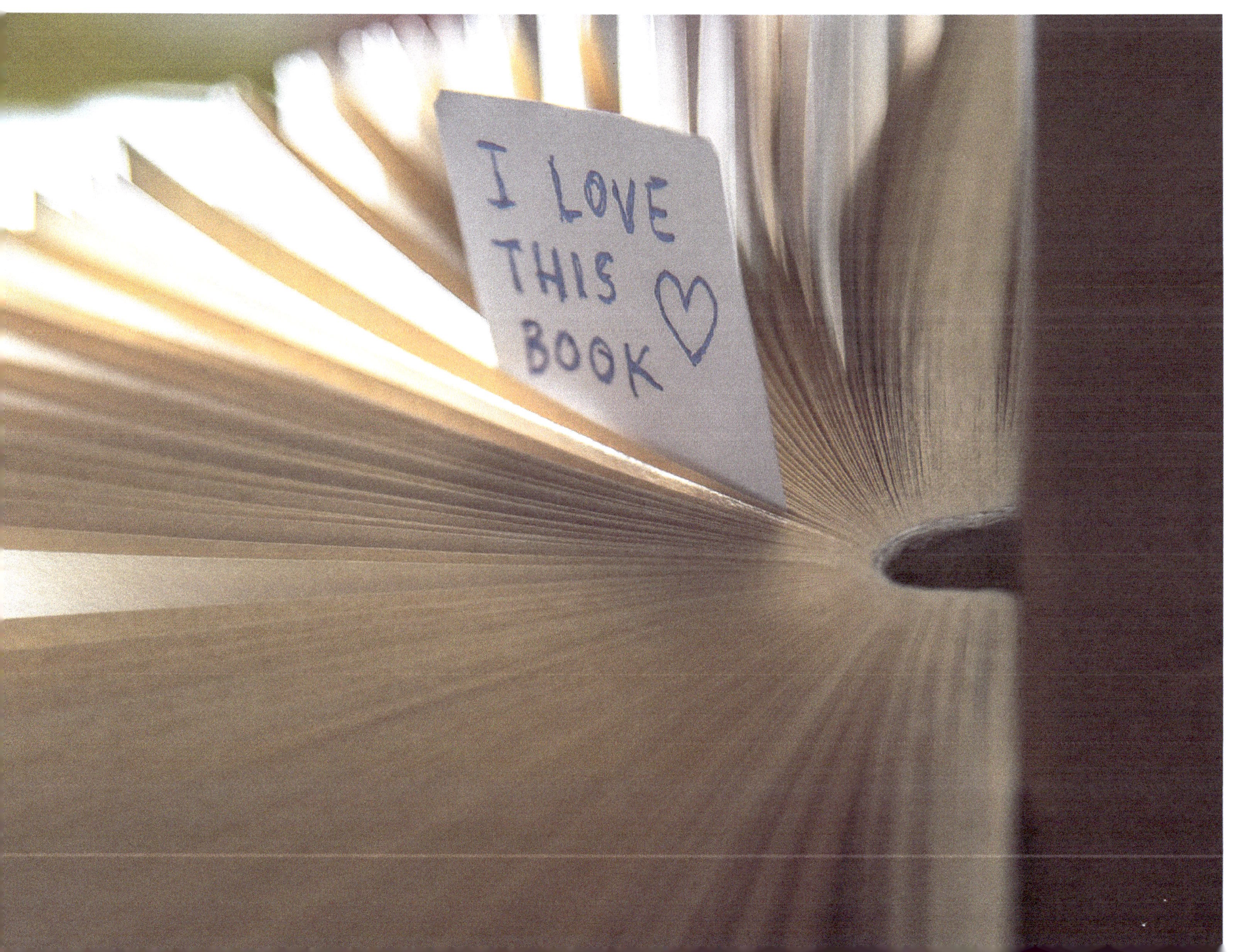
I LOVE
THIS
BOOK

# CALENDARS

No matter how the times progress, you always need to know what day it is! See what unique calendars you can make for your desk or office!

# CANDLES

Sure, you can't make candles themselves with your Cricut. But you could get a candle in a blank glass holder and put something PERFECT for any occasion on the outside of it. These make ideal gifts, let me tell you.

# CANVAS TOTE BAGS

Tote bags are one of the most useful accessories on the planet. Keep all your things together and add some style with your Cricut! Heck, if you felt like it, you could get some canvas and make your tote bag!

# CAR DECALS

Got a business? Tell the world about it as you travel through your week!

# CENTERPIECES

Any large-scale event could benefit from themed centerpieces to amuse and wow your guests!



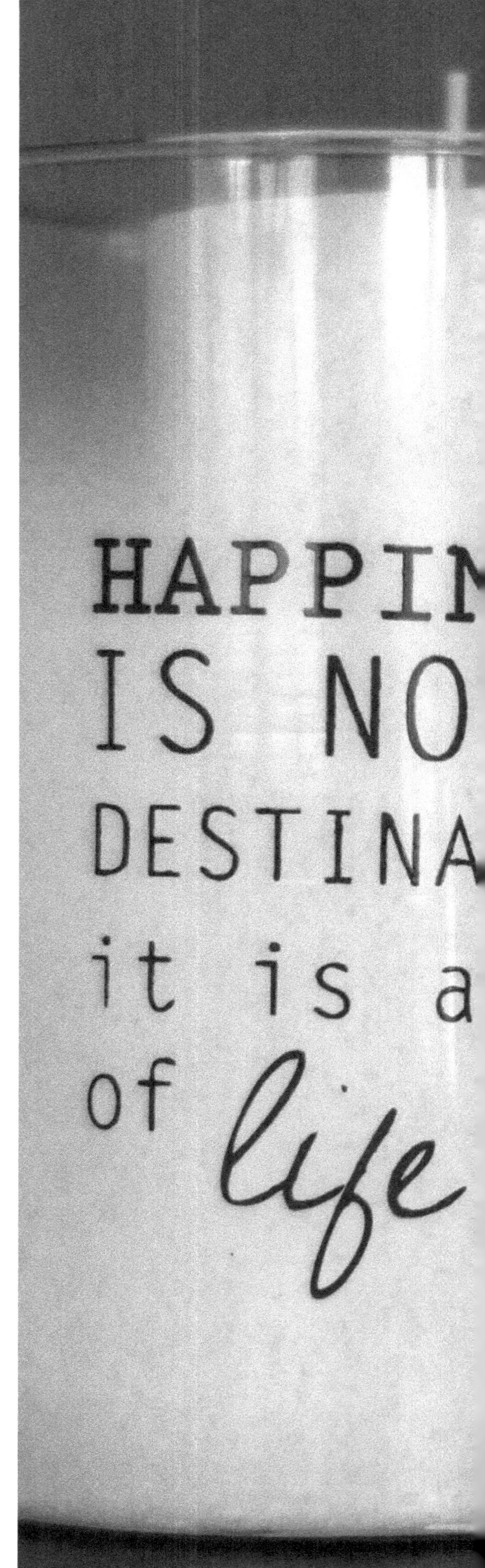

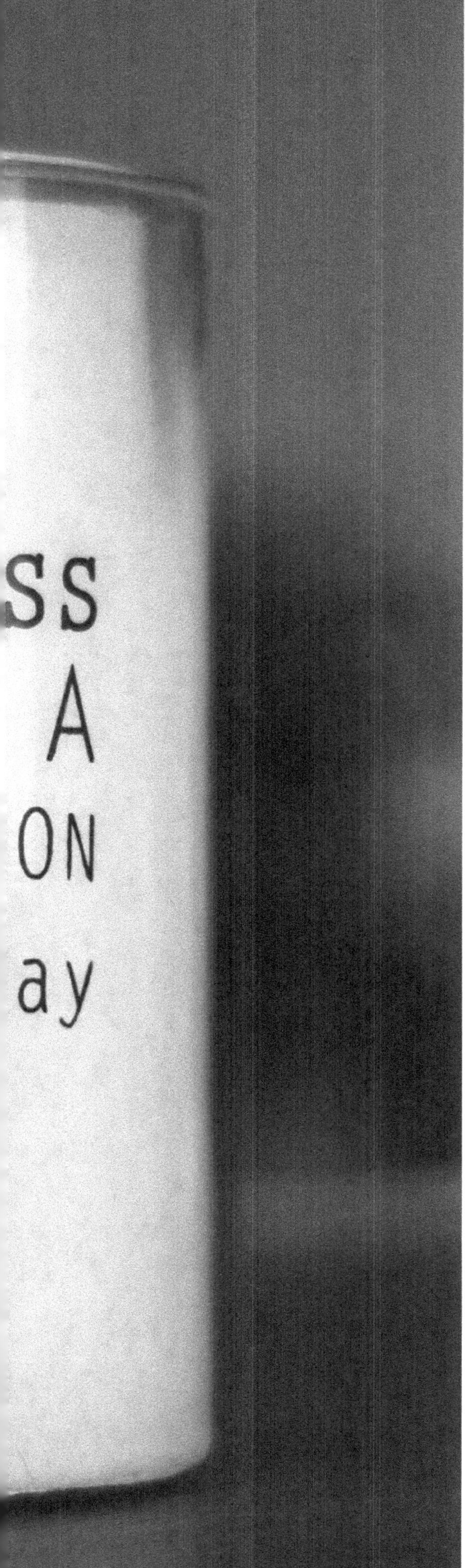


## CLOTHING

Put your creative flourish on anything you own with Cricut joy and the numerous materials they have to offer. Whether it's an iron-on decal or a fabric embellishment, there's no shortage of ways to impress!

## COASTERS

Like so many other things in this list, coasters can make such a great gift for housewarming or holidays. Everyone could use a unique set of coasters to keep their surfaces safe and dry!

## COFFEE MUGS

Coffee mugs are probably the one dish that I will always want more when I see them in my house. They're great for so many things, and having unique ones, you are the perfect addition to any office or kitchen.

## COLORING PAGES

Using the pen in your Cricut, you can download line art to make coloring pages of any style or theme for yourself or your loved ones! If you have children in your family coming to visit, this makes for a great group activity!

## COMMEMORATIVE PLATES

Did you know that come Cricut materials that can adhere to ceramic could make an excellent embellishment for decorative commemorative plates? What occasions could you commemorate?

## CRAFT FOAM SHAPE SETS

Just like with the puzzle sets, you can cut just about any shape you want out of craft foam. Doing so on the foam sheets with an adhesive backing could allow you to make your own little crafting sets of any theme you desire! It includes letters as well!

## DECORATIVE PLAQUES

Decorative plaques are a breeze, and as you gain more competence with the Cricut system, you can get more intricate and creative!

## DIY CRAFT KITS

Making crafting kit components with the Cricut is a breeze. Let your imagination run wild on what pieces you could bundle together for someone to make their crafting projects! Let your mind run wild on this one as they make lovely party favors, gifts for children or crafters, and so much more!

## DIY DECALS

The decals you create can place onto a carrier or backing sheet to give out. If you don't want to put your decal right onto something, simply top it with a piece of transfer tape and give it away!



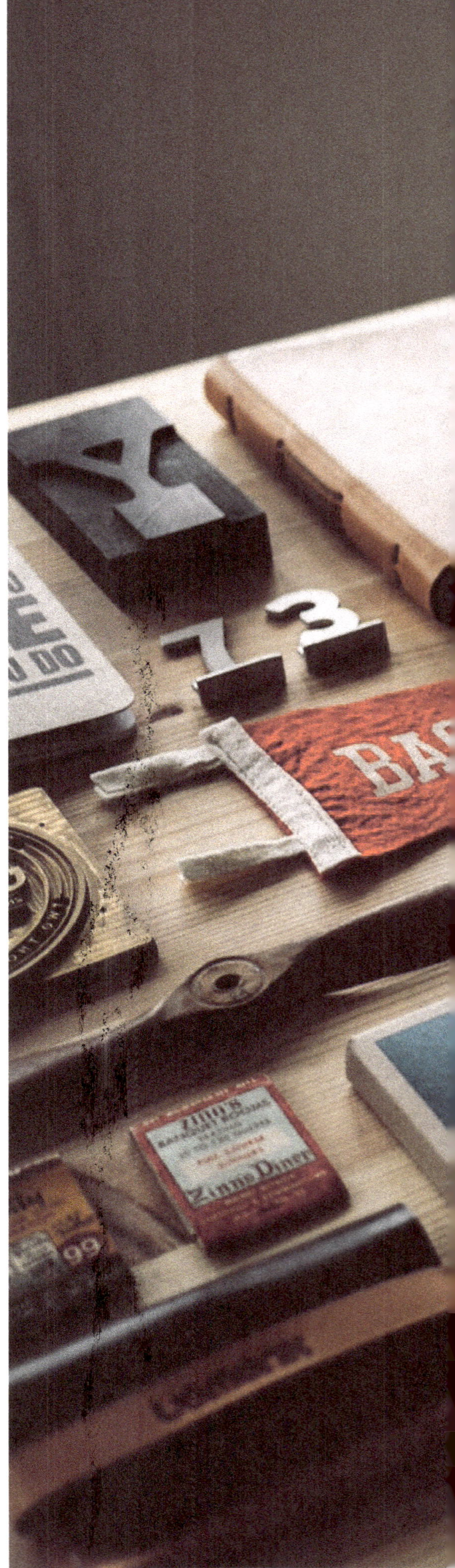

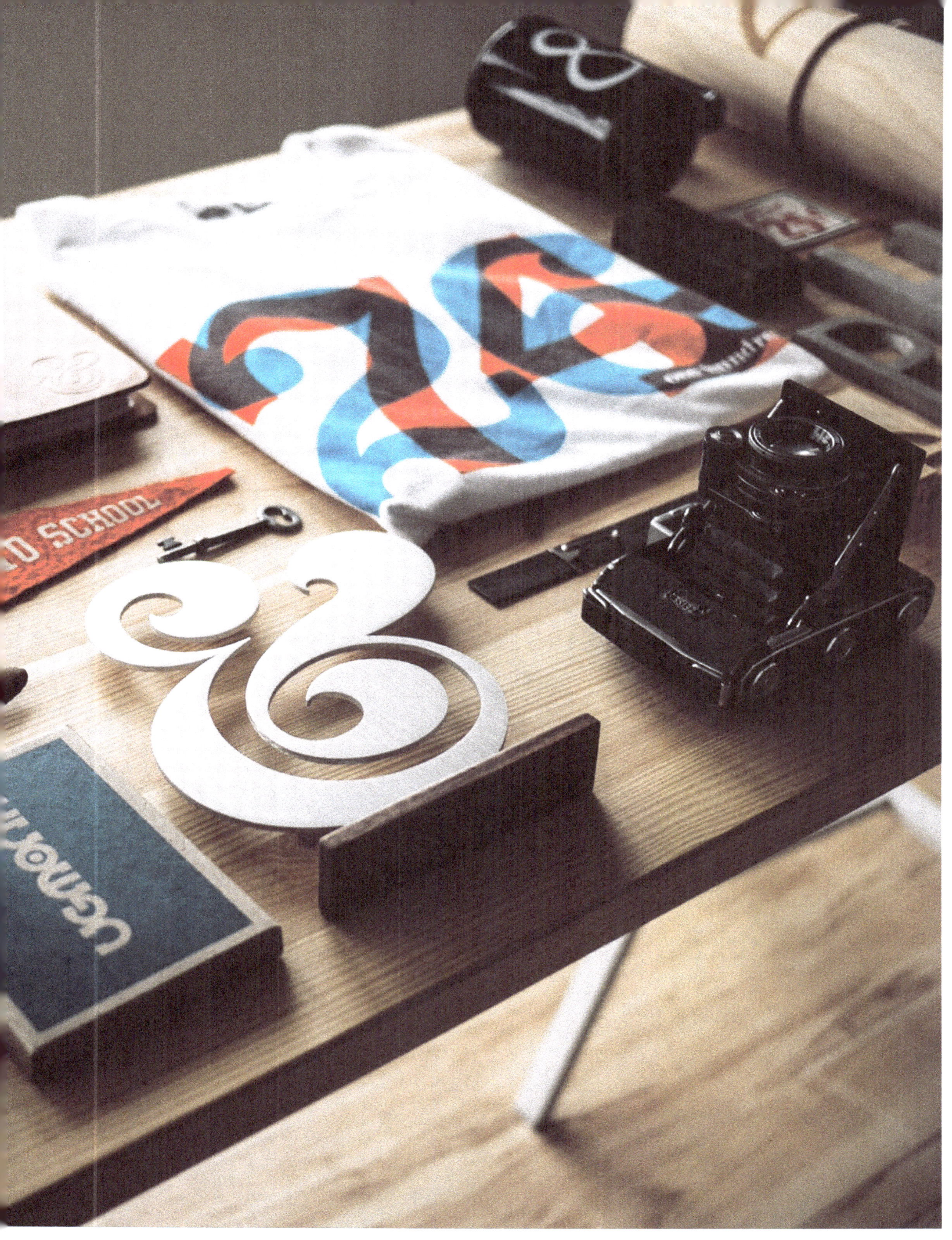

## DOILIES

Cricut's intricate designs can allow you to make doilies of so many different materials, colors, sizes, shapes, themes, and more!

## ENVELOPES

Did you know that envelopes make out of one continuous piece of paper that cuts, folded, and glued in a specific way? It means that you can take any piece of paper you like, with any print you want, and make an envelope out of it! Go nuts!

## FLOWERPOTS

A flowerpot can be sort of a mundane piece. However, with some craft paint and a stencil that you made with your Cricut, or with a decal, they can transform into something that fits your décor perfectly!

## FRAMED AFFIRMATIONS

This life is tough! Affirmations that you can put in your font or style can make all the difference in the vibe you get from a personal space. Jazz up your own and put them all over your room!

## GIFT CARD ENVELOPES

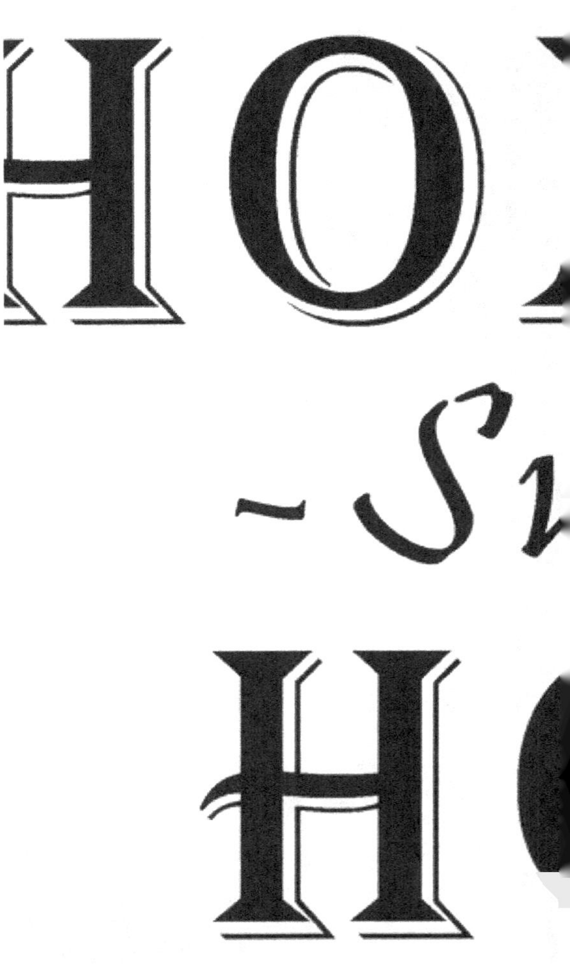

These can do with scrapbooking paper, construction paper, foil paper, or anything. You can elevate this tiny little gift into something truly personal that anyone would love to have.

## GIFT TAGS

Going that little extra bit toward making someone's gift look and feel unique does make a difference.

## GREETING CARDS

Some of the gorgeous greeting cards at the supermarket these days can run you about $9 per card! With the materials to hand in your crafting station, you can make cards that are just gorgeous, multi-layered, and make them carry your message. It makes the whole gift so much more personal and meaningful.

## HATS

There are patterns to make your hats and decals you can make that will make an existing hat pop!

## HOLIDAY DÉCOR

I can't even be honest with you about how nuts I've gone into this category. You can make so many decorations for any occasion that you just can't even imagine doing all of them for every holiday!

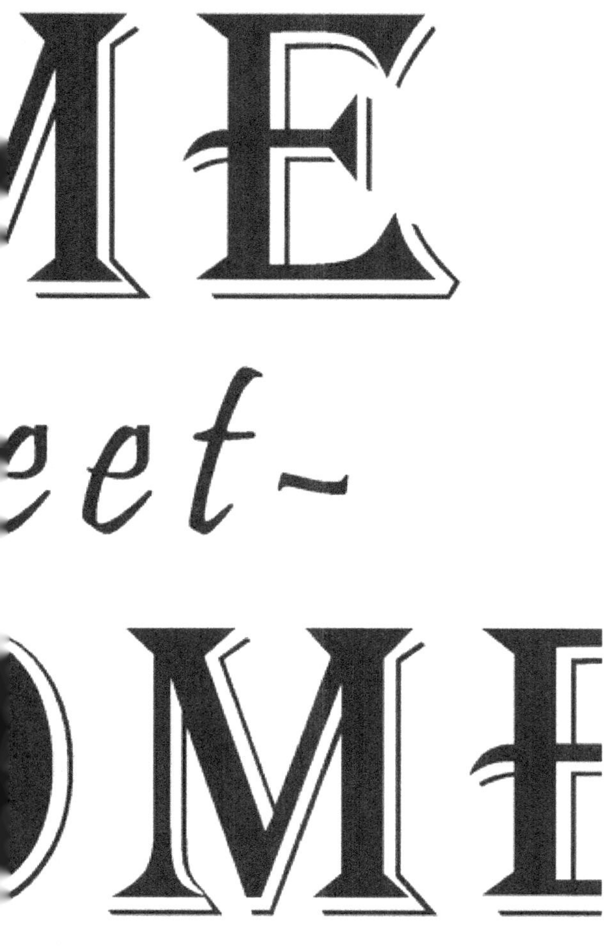

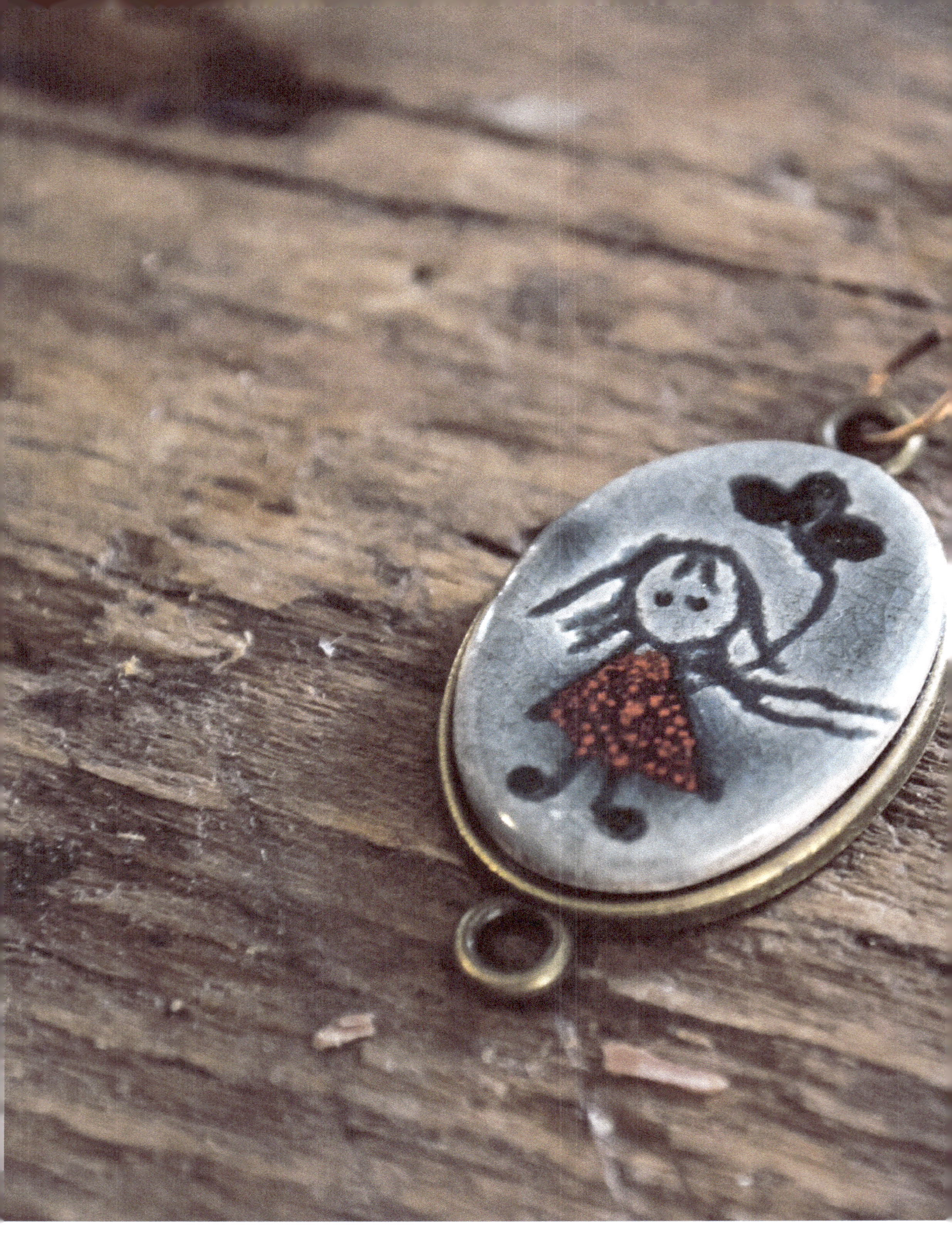

## HOODIES

Nothing is more comforting than a nice thick hoodie, sometimes. Put your personal touch on a hoodie or carry around the mark of your favorite characters or phrases.

## JEWELRY

Oh yes. You can make your jewelry with the materials available through Cricut. Leather, fabric, metal. It's all there.

## KEEPSAKE BOXES

No craft is complete if it can't, in some way, be tied back to keepsake boxes, right? They're all over the crafting world, and you can absolutely make keepsake boxes or just decorate them to the nines!

## KEY FOBS

Make your keys stand out by making an adorable or stylish fey fob!

## KEYCHAINS

Got a favorite character or emoji? Make a keychain!
Labeled Kitchenware
From canisters to kitchen cracks, there's nothing you can't decal!

# LABELS

If an organization is your forte, using Cricut can help you make gorgeous labels for every room of the house!

# LANYARDS

Keep your keys or ID cards displayed with style and comfort.

# LEATHER ACCENTS

From scrapbooking to home décor, leather accents can elevate your designs from looking great to looking thoroughly professional.

# LEATHER ACCESSORIES

Wristbands, wallets, lanyards, wallets, etc. Your Cricut can transform sheets of leather into your most gorgeous, stylish accessories.

# LUGGAGE TAGS

Never be unsure of which bag on the carousel is you. Make a luggage tag that stands apart from the crowd as much as you do and claims your pocket in no time!

# MAGNETIC POETRY SETS

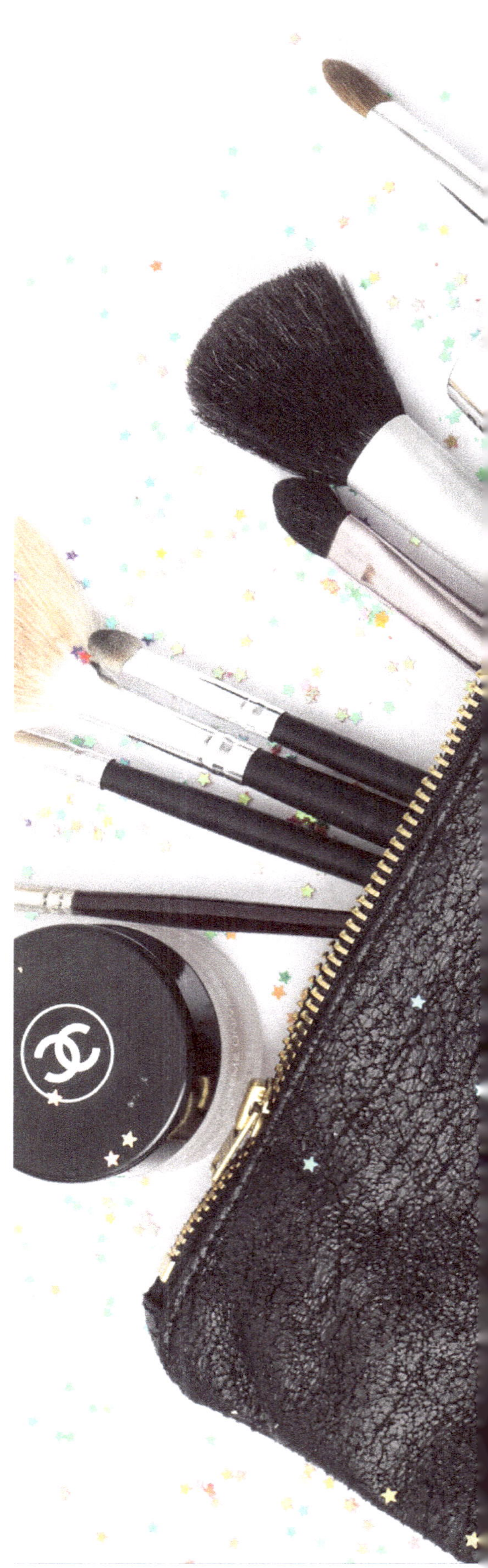

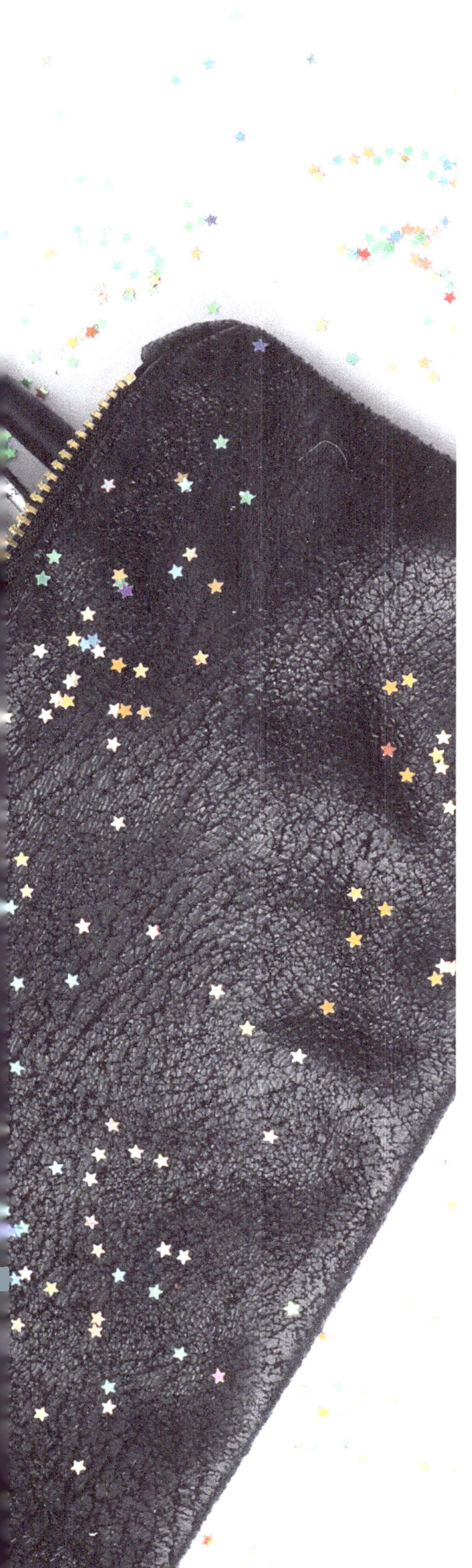

By printing words onto a set of printable magnets, you can create a group to make magnetic poems and limericks on your doors, refrigerators, or metal tables!

## MAGNETIC PUZZLES

Puzzles are a timeless gift that is always fun. Print a picture of a loved one onto a printable magnet, make a jigsaw puzzle, and create a beautiful setting for the front of your refrigerator or a friend!

## MAKEUP BAGS

Personalizing a simple zippered bag can make all the difference in the style of that item! Make it yours! You could even make your zippered bag with your Cricut and then decorate it!

## MANDALA DECALS

Mandalas are gorgeous, and Cricut is the perfect tool to help you make decals to put on just about anything.

# Chapter 2
# Making Your First Project
# Idea

According to the instruction, there will be directions on your screen that you must follow to create your first project after setting up your Cricut joy machine. You will still be using the link you found on the paper when setting up your device. If you have not yet received your machine and are interested in knowing how it works, or you are looking for extra clarifications, here's what it will say.

## First Step

First off, load a pen into the accessories clamp. You can pick whichever color you think will go best with the paper you have received. Next, you want to turn the knob so that the indicator is pointed to "cardstock," considering what you will be working with. Have you had a good look at your mats yet? The blue rug is what you will want to use for this project. You should remove the plastic cover - keep it, don't throw it away as you will need to recover your mat when you're done to avoid dust accumulation - and lay down the paper on the mat with the top left corners of the material and the grid aligned.

## Second Step

Make sure that the paper is pressed flat before you push it between the rollers firmly. The mat has to rest on the bottom roller. When it is in place, press the "Load" button

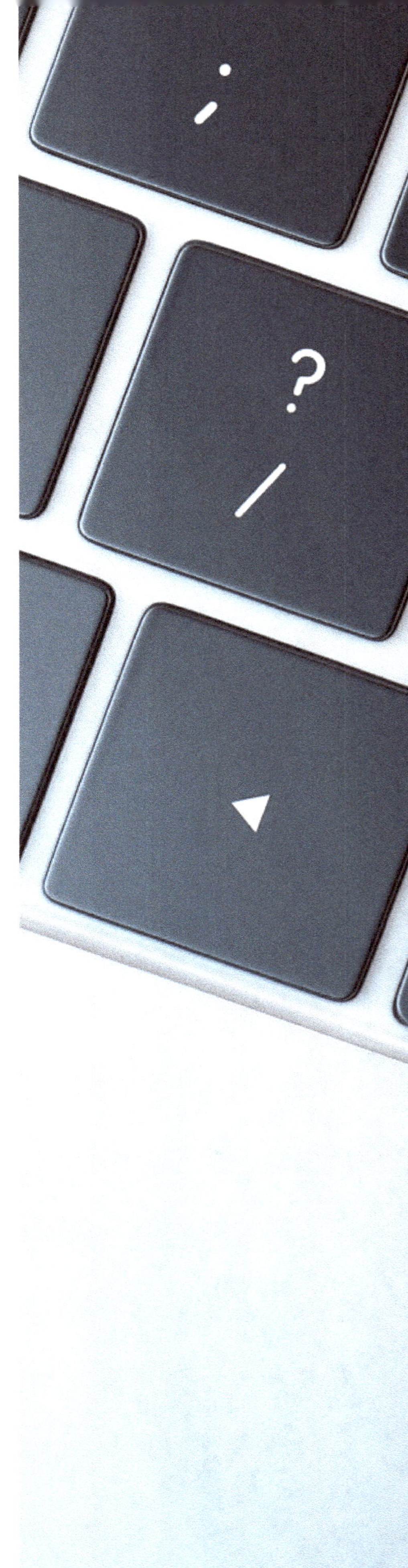

enter
return
CREATE

to load your mat between the rollers. Press "go," which will be flashing at this stage; wait for the machine to work its magic on your project. Once everything is done, the light will flash, and you can press the "Load" button again to unload the mat. Your paper will still be sticking to the mat when you remove it .

# Third Step

Be careful when removing the material from the mat. Don't be too hasty; take your time so that it doesn't tear. Pull the meat away from the cardstock instead of doing it the other way around. After completing that step, you can now fold the cardstock in half, insert the liners into the card's corner slots, and it's done!

You have just made your first ever Cricut project in a matter of minutes from start to finish! Congratulations! What are you waiting for? Do more projects! There are a ton of templates you can play around with-practice, practice, practice.

When starting a new project, you must always keep in mind that you must first have all of the materials necessary to complete the project. It is still helpful to check your stock of tools and materials before getting started. The worst feeling is when you sit down and begin working on a complex project to realize you are out of a specific material needed to finish the job. It will save you a lot of time in the long run if you spend a few minutes at the beginning taking stock of your inventory! Working with materials you already have on hand is also a great way to keep your crafting costs low. It will always feel good to know that you made a custom piece



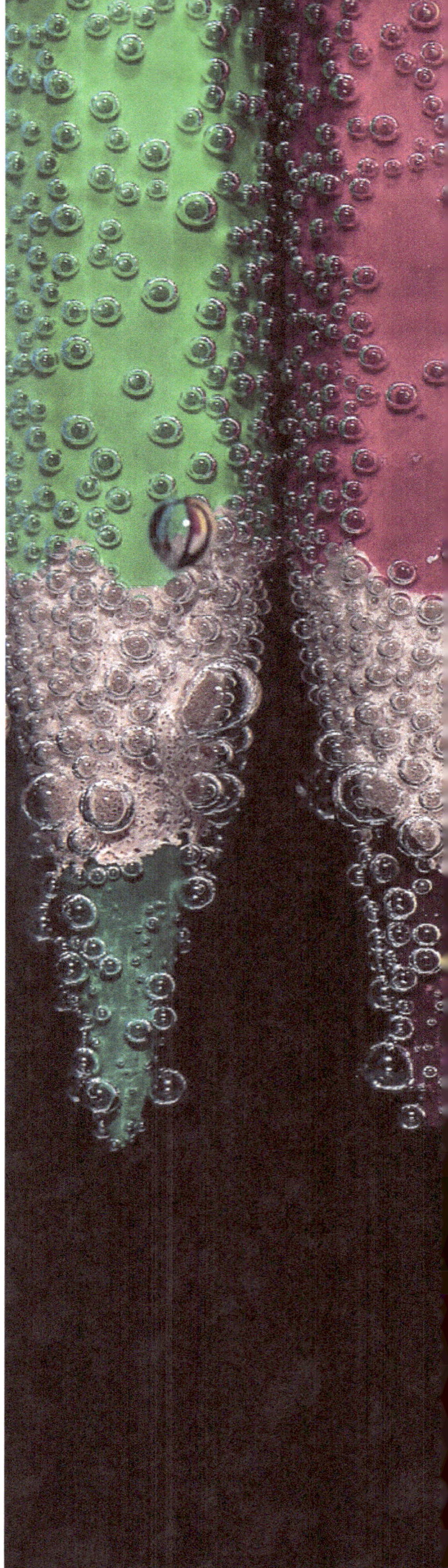

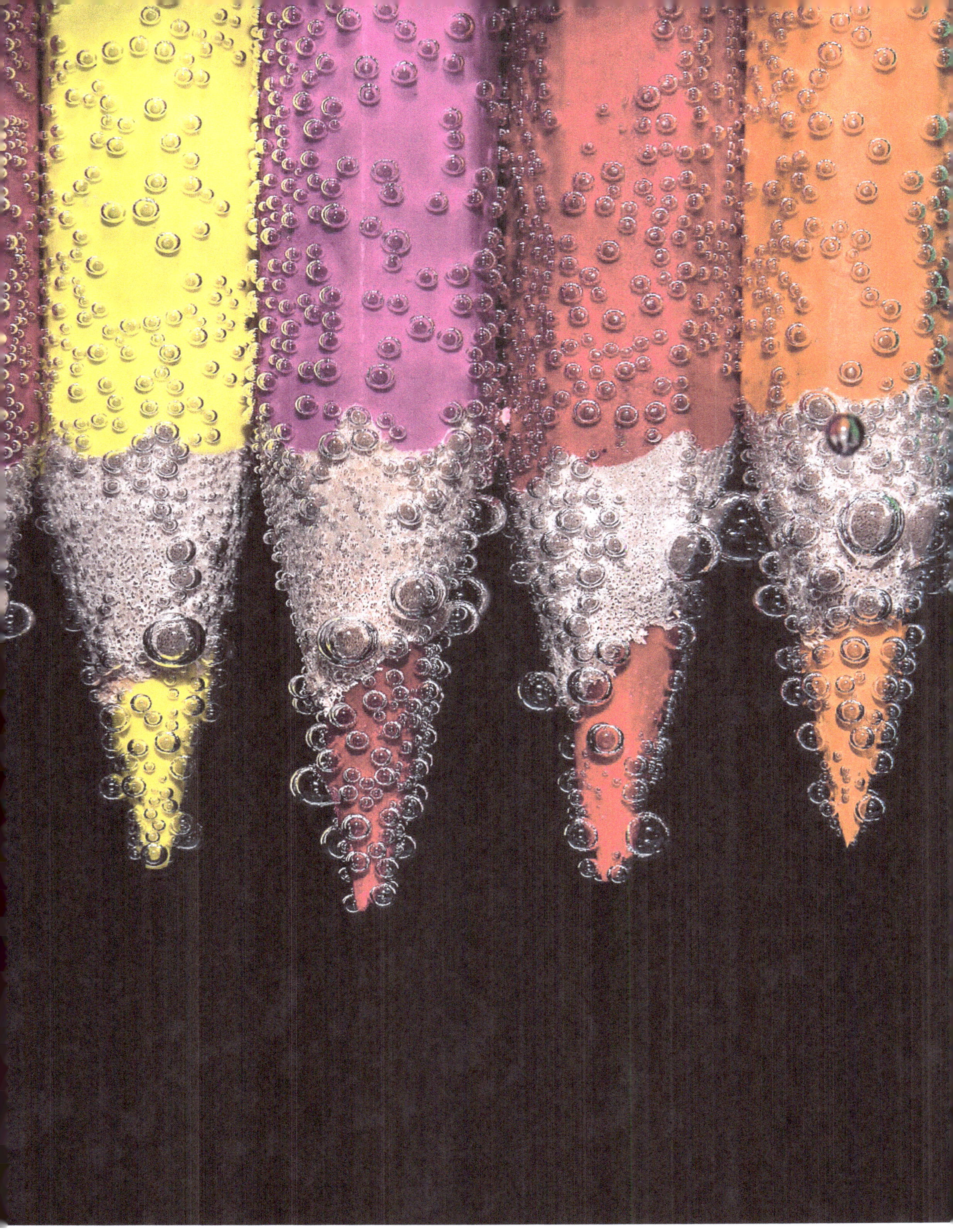

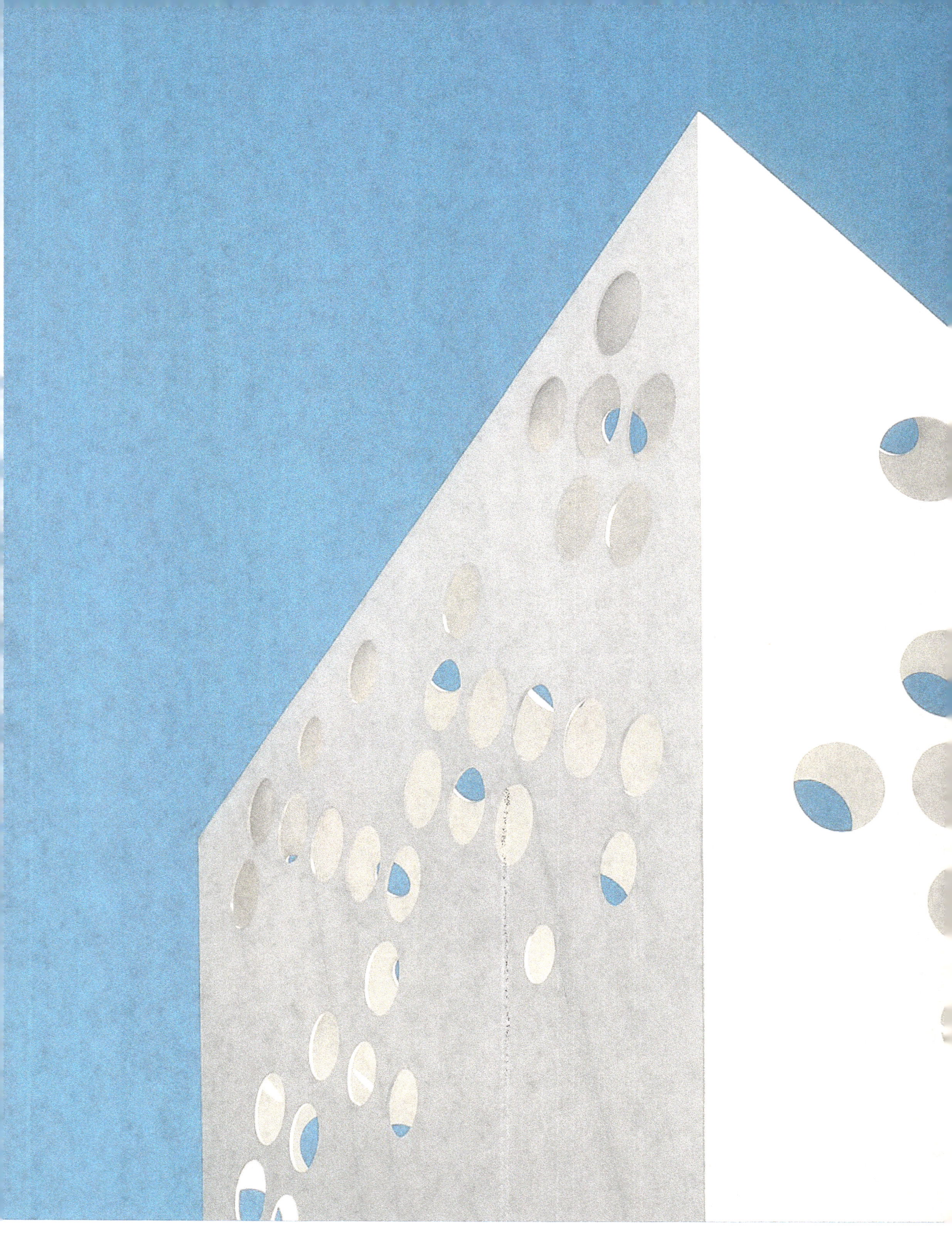

of work without spending a ton of extra money just to complete it!

# How to Upload Images with A Cricut Joy

For this method to operate, you will need to upload a picture from your desktop. Click complicated once you upload it, and the next window is where the magic takes place.

At the left corner of the top. Look at the wand? Click on it and press on the hair. Click on the continuation button and name the picture. Click the save button.

It's gone, and it's been so simple. Now, let's look after her flesh.

First, press back on the magic wand to remove the face, arms, body, and any hard-to-reach pieces. Once you've finished that, take the eraser to wash the remainder of your flesh until it's gone.

Click Continue, identify your picture, and then press Save when the image is to your liking.

Insert both pictures into the surface of your Cricut Design Space. You can bring them back together once you've got them there. I'm excited about this process because sometimes, like the hair color, I want to change things. I couldn't change the hair color if I left the picture like it was. But I can do that now.

Would you like to know how to edit images in Cricut Design Space as thrilled as I am? I pray so.

Now, go out and do some crafting!

# Chapter 3
# How to use Design Space in Cricut Joy

Upon learning about the tools, accessories, software, and functionalities of the Cricut Joy, it'd be unfair not to understand the general cutting process since it may be something foreign to most users looking for their first plotter. Unlike manual tools such as the Big Shot, the Cricut Joy cutting plotter is always linked to cutting software, which is why we must work with them from our computer, tablet, or mobile phone.

The necessary cutting process with the Cricut Joy always starts from the software we create or download our design and send it to be cut to the machine. However, before cutting, we must do at least two essential things; the first and most logical, load the material into the device through its cutting mat and configure the cutting settings according to the material we want to cut. Each material requires a suitable blade depth, pressure force, and cutting speed.

Many of these concepts may be completely unknown to you, but I intend that at the end of the comparison, you fully understand how each of the machines works to choose the one that best suits your needs.

# The Design Program

If we consider that the great advantage of having a cutting plotter instead of a die-cutting machine like the Big Shot is the capacity to cut and personalized designs, the design software with which the machine works is a fundamental point to consider. Far beyond the quality of each one's cuts, the software makes the real difference between the two brands, which is why we'll analyze them in-depth. But before delving more profound, we will have to see its essential characteristics.

# The Cricut Joy Design Space

The Cricut Joy works with an online application called Design Space. It is accessed from the HTTP // design. Cricut. Although it does not require a complete installation on the computer, it will ask you to download and install its plugin. As it is an online application, you can access it from any computer with an internet connection, and it is no longer available the moment you lose that connection. In the past, the Cricut app could only be used in English, but as of May 2019, it can be used in different languages and users.

Despite being an online application, it also requires minimum requirements to work with it, and since the summer of 2019, it begins to display messages

warning that it will stop working in Windows 7.

How about being inside all the secrets inside the Cricut program? It was thinking of you that we decided to make a sequence of contents exclusively focused on the curiosities and applications of your Cricut.

# How to use Cricut Design Space

Already, you know that with the help of the Cricut program. Design Space has the images necessary to awaken your creative instinct. But how have you used these images inside the tool?

The Design Space platform is complete, it allows you to create an image before purchasing, so you can be sure that it will be the most suitable for your project. Also, you can upload your pictures and crop them with your Cricut Joy.

# How to Edit Images in Design Space

First of all, you must agree that having such a functional application helps a lot when it comes to being inspired and doing a job as beautiful as those present in the tool. There are thousands of options available for you to use in your creations.

When starting a new project, you will access the "images" option within the Cricut program. There are thousands of image options that Design Space offers. You can search within a category for something that is by your project.

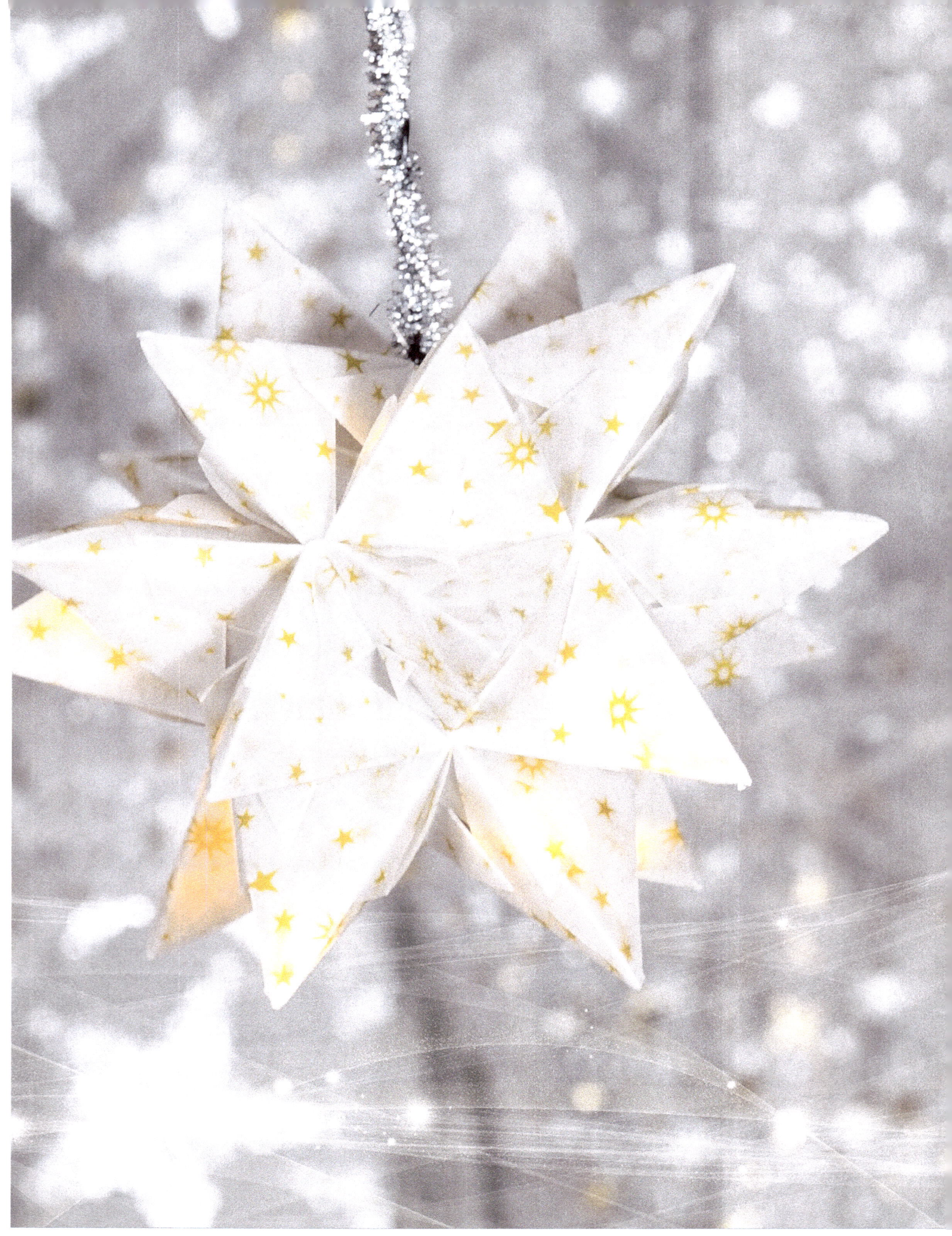

If you want to select more than one image option to work, hold the "CTRL" option on the keyboard and fix the images you want. Before starting the project, if you change your mind, to delete the selection, just click on the image again or on the "x" in the lower right corner, where the thumbnail image is.

Opening the selected images, note that you have several assembled segments in the upper right corner in the "layers" option that are part of the image's overall composition.

It is essential to pay attention to them because it is from these layers that it will be possible to edit the size, colors, and shape of each of the project's components.

When selecting a part of the image layer, you can change its settings, one of which is the design color. To do this, choose which elements you want, go to the upper left corner in the "path" option and define the most suitable color for your project.

Remember, if you want to edit all the image elements, just select all the layers.

In the same "path" class, you also have the option of defining different types of shapes for your project. They range from cutting, drawing, stamping, stamping, engraving, curling, and drilling. All of this depends a lot on which project you want to develop. The exciting thing is that you can see how the image will look when completed.

That way, having edited and selected the way you want to work with your Cricut, the next step is to observe how your Cricut will work on the image components.

But what if you want to save material?

Well, so that the components of layers do not separate while creating the project, go to the upper right corner, in the part of the screen, and choose the option "attach."

Thus, this option ensures that the layers are merged and the components are grouped correctly during the item's manufacturing process. This option is recommended for those who will work with image printing or drawing, followed by clipping.

# How to Upload Basic Images to Design Space

Many people prefer to work with author projects, so they have doubts about using the tool to turn their ideas into reality. The process may seem complicated, but you will see that it is not! Just follow me on these simple steps. We will first use simple images with few components.

In the initial screen of your new project, in the option "upload," you can upload images for free (essential and vector) in the formats that are informed by the software. Just click on "load image" and select the desired file. Note that the Cricut program offers three options related to the type of image, i.e., its complexity. The more colors, details, and layers you have in your vision, the more complicated it is. Therefore, you choose the option best suited to that. Bearing in mind that complexity selects the best tools to be worked according to each image.

The next step is to edit the image if you want to modify certain aspects. In this example, note that we removed the heart's red background; this is possible for all images that have low complexity of details. You can make the background transparent in a single color. Bearing in mind that we have chosen the most strai-



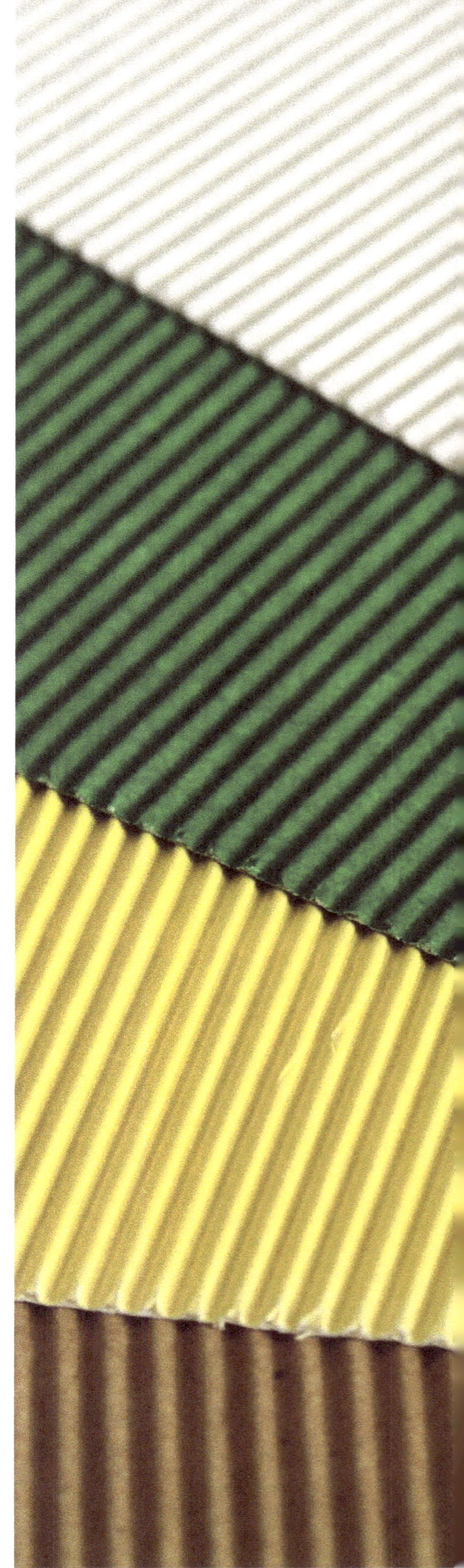

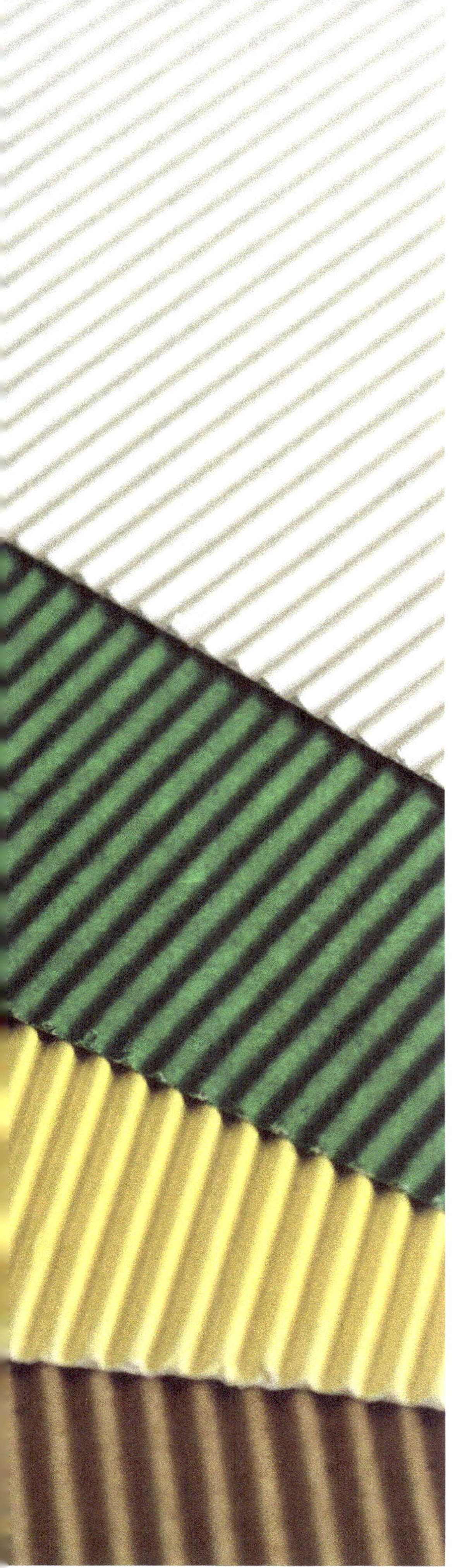

ghtforward option of all.

Also, there are other options, which you can delete components and crop the image.

Then, having edited the image the way you want, you will be redirected to this stage, in which you must choose the type of purpose your project is intended for and how it will be, visibly in each of them.

For example, in the first option, where you will save as an image to print and cut, some details of the background are still visible, so for the sake of aesthetics, we will choose the second option because the final components can be changed when editing Image.

Saving, you will always find your image in this space. To start bringing your project to life, just insert and go to the last step.

Finally, it's left to your creativity. As you saw in the previous tutorial, you can change your image's shape, size, and color. Also, you can rotate to form different shapes, and if you want the design to remain during the making, attach.

## How about Cricut Access?

Cricut Access is Cricut's monthly subscription that gives you access (hence its name) to many Cricut Design Space resources: projects, images, fonts, etc.

A few months ago, it was activating your free subscription or signing up for Access was a complicated task. And, in fact, it still cannot be accessed from the computer.

But, for some time now, it has been possible to quickly sign up for Cricut Access from our mobile phone or tablet. To do this, we just have to install the Cricut Design Space application on our device, either Android or Apple, and follow the steps.

## FOR ANDROID.

You have to go to the main menu, click on "Cricut Access," and follow the steps. From there, Google takes care of managing your subscription.

## FOR IOS

If, instead of Android, your device is an iPhone or an iPad, the steps to follow are the same., once activated, Apple will manage your subscription, and you can do it from the settings menu of your device.

## BUY DESIGNS

If what you need is to buy Cricut designs, do it also from your mobile. The amount will be charged in the payment system you have configured for your device, either in Google Play or in the App Store. In this way, your payments will not only be safe but also a sea of simplicity. Just follow the cutting steps in Cricut Design Space, and when it's time to pay, the app will send the bill directly to Google or Apple. Do not worry! Before you confirm it, it will ask you, and no purchases will be made alone as if by magic.

## ONCE YOU HAVE PURCHASED THE DESIGN, YOU WILL HAVE IT ACCESSIBLE FROM ANY DEVICE.

As long as you have your access subscription active, you can use all these resources for free as many times as

you want; however, you will have to pay for each image or font you want to use the moment you unsubscribe. So, if you had saved a project in which you had used an image or access source, and you want to cut it again after your subscription ends, you will have to pay for those elements.

As you can see, the subscriptions also include discounts on your purchases on the Cricut website. However, it must be remembered that their machine and accessories store still does not ship to Europe, so you will only be able to enjoy those advantages to buy designs.

# How to Find Cricut Access Resources

All the elements included in Cricut access are correctly identified in Design Space with the icon of the [a]. And, also, in the case of images and projects, you can filter the results so that only those included in your access subscription are shown. In the following pictures, you can see how to identify the products included in access and filter them.

## PROJECTS

As you can see, Cricut access gives you access to a lot of free resources that can make your life much easier when doing your projects.

# How to Save and Share Files on Cricut Joy

Saving and sharing files is one of those things that, at

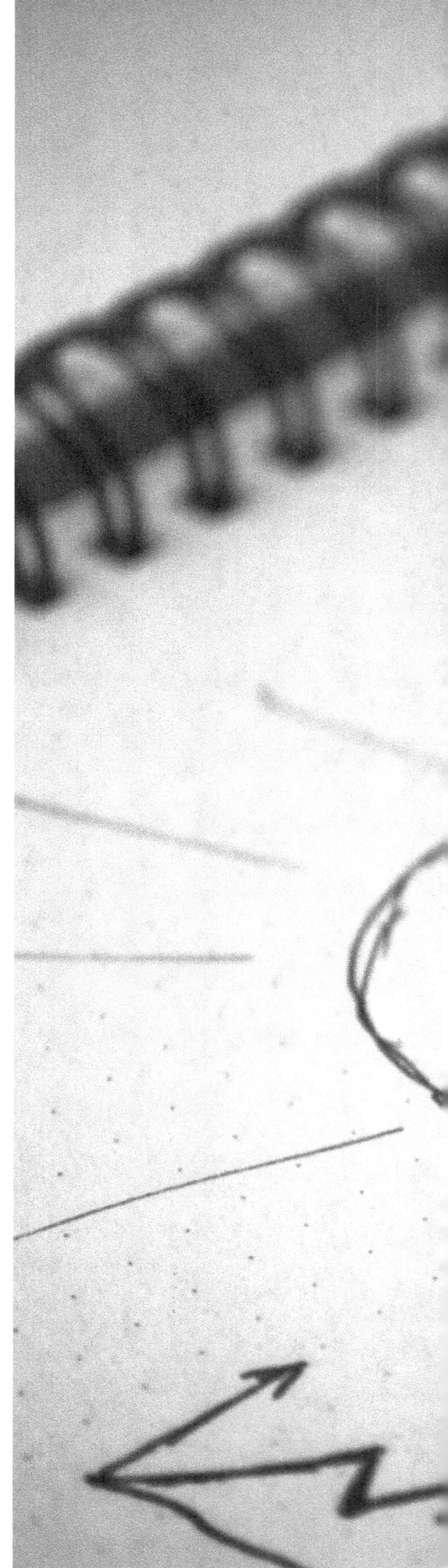

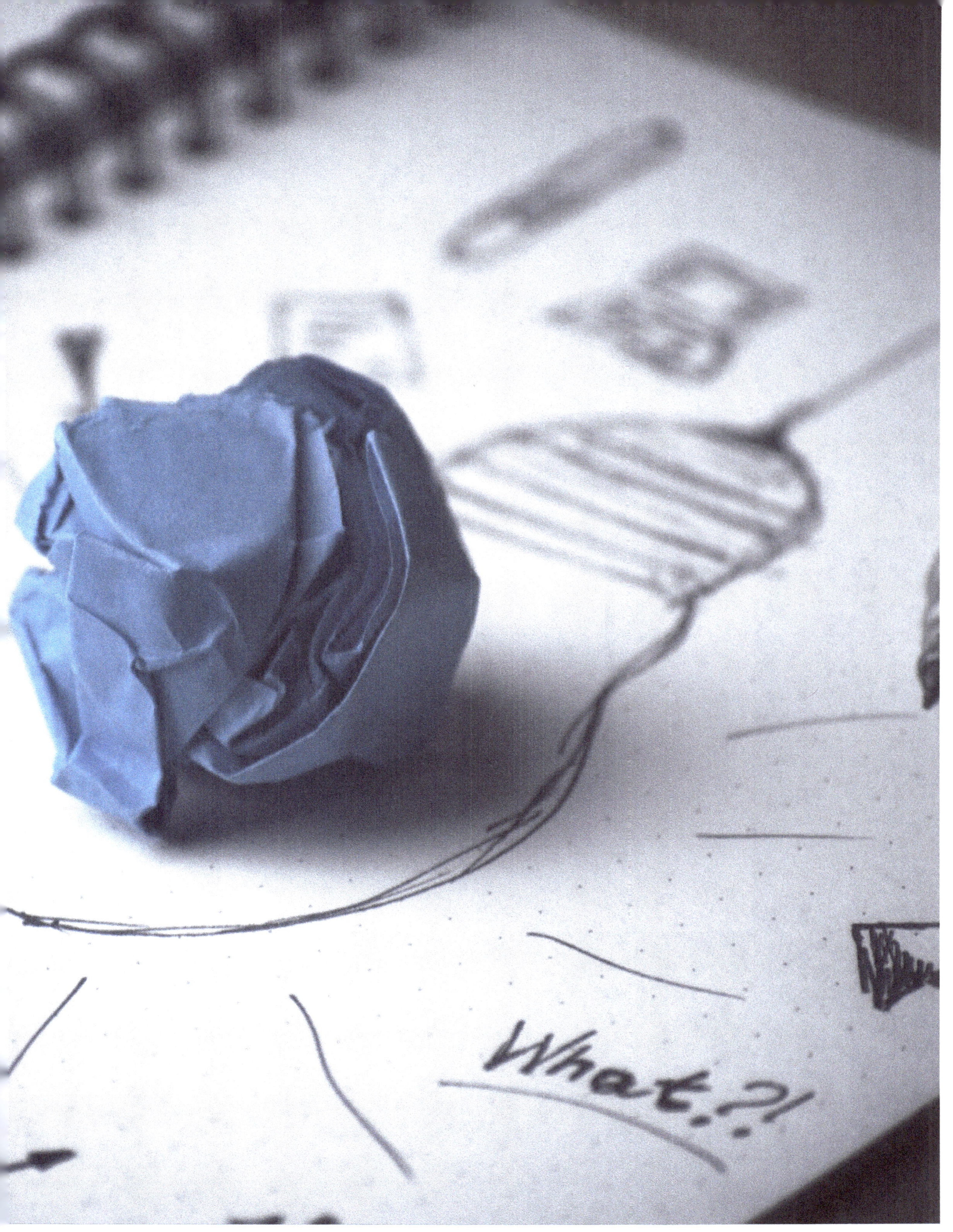
What.?!

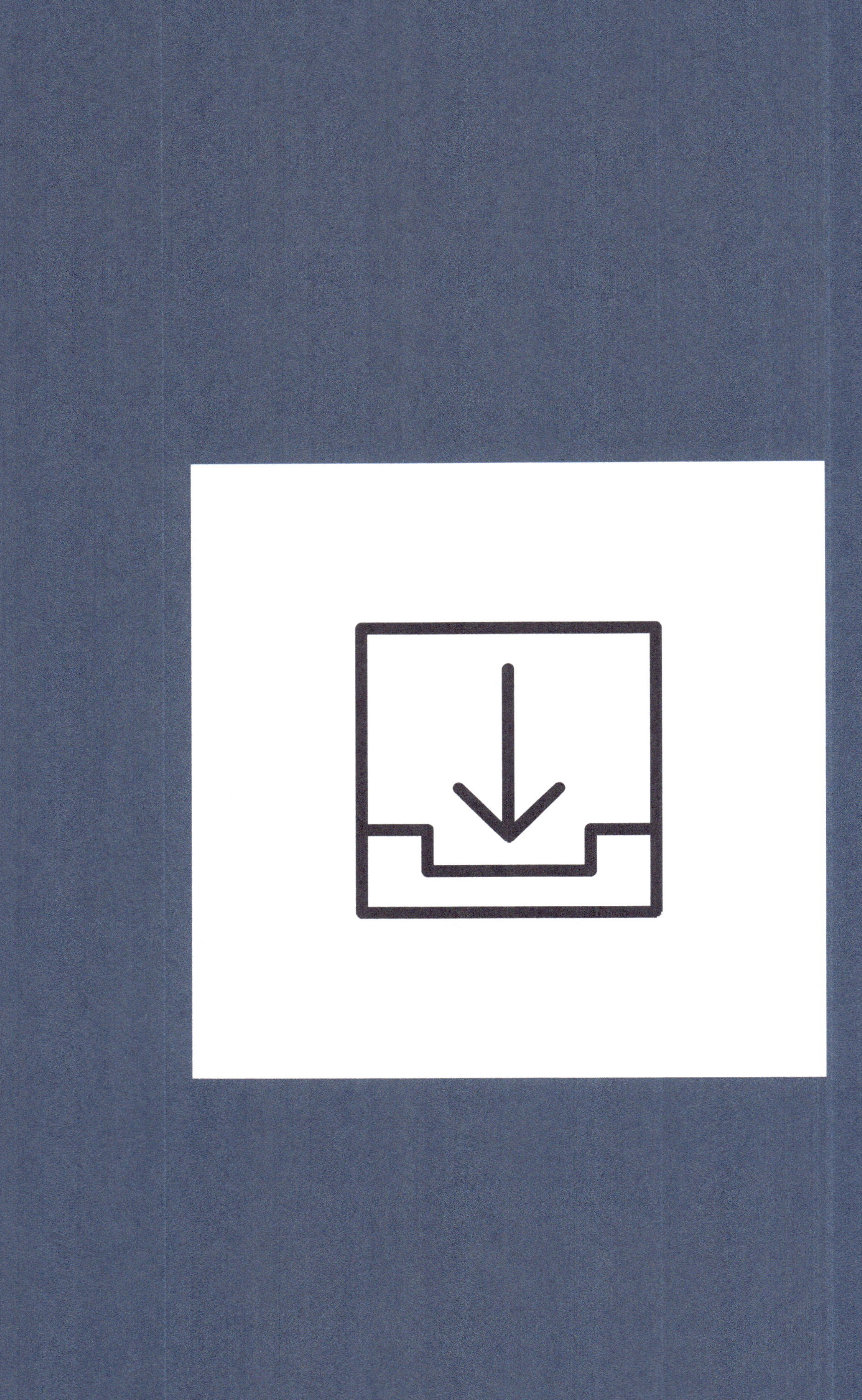

first, nobody thinks about, but that later can bring you more of a headache. Sometimes only because you want to use your designs on another computer, others because you want to share the design with a friend or client, and others, just because you are farsighted and want to have a backup of all your projects. So, let's try to explain what you can and cannot do in Cricut Design Space.

## SAVE FILES

As you already know, Cricut machines work with Cricut Design Space. This implies that you can access them from any device connected to the network by simply clicking on your account. However, we will not be able to work on our designs offline.

From " My projects," you have access to all the saved projects, but also, any image that you upload to the "program" is stored so that you can use it at any time.

The fact that everything is automatically saved to your online account means that you will not download a file as such to your computer.

If you are interested in saving only one capture image, you can always use a virtual printer or a screen capture to save it. Still, you will not be able to download a vector file (such as an SVG) to, for example, cut it with another machine other than Cricut Joy.

## SHARE FILES

Our Cricut projects, in principle, are private, and only we can see them. But we have the option to "Share" to share some of them publicly and be used by anyone. Here you can see what we have shared for now. And you can access all the projects shared by other users from the «Cricut Community« section. One thing that's admirable about Cricut Shared Projects is that you can put photos of the final result and leave a description. This way, it is much more attractive to other users, and you can take a lot of ideas from other projects.

## Limitations

### PROJECTS CANNOT BE DOWNLOADED

As we have seen, in Cricut's world, everything is within your account, and that has its advantages and disadvantages. The main advantage is for designers, as it prevents hacking to a great extent. First of all, because of not being able to download the files for use outside of Design Space, there is no risk of buying, downloading, and distributing them without permission.

### EACH PROJECT HAS LINKED ALL THE IMAGES THAT HAVE BEEN USED.

The second thing to keep in mind is that when a user saves their project, the images and designs that they have used are linked to the project. If you look at the project's description, the pictures that have been used to do it, and the price also appear. Therefore, anyone who wants to do a similar project user will have to buy the same images that she has

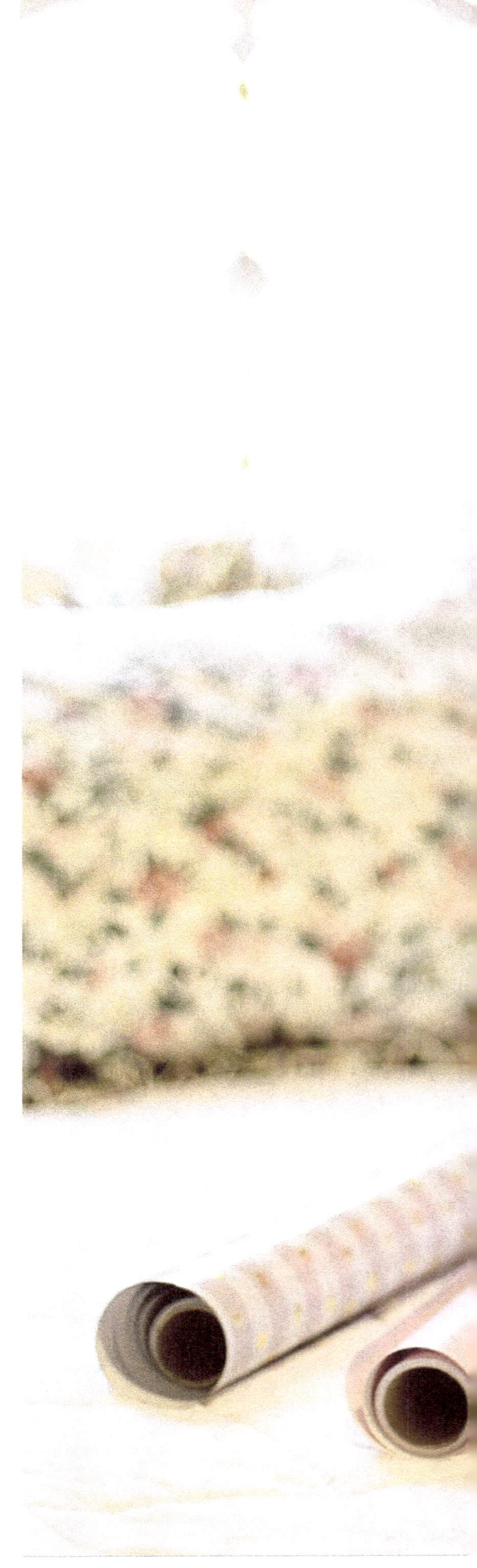

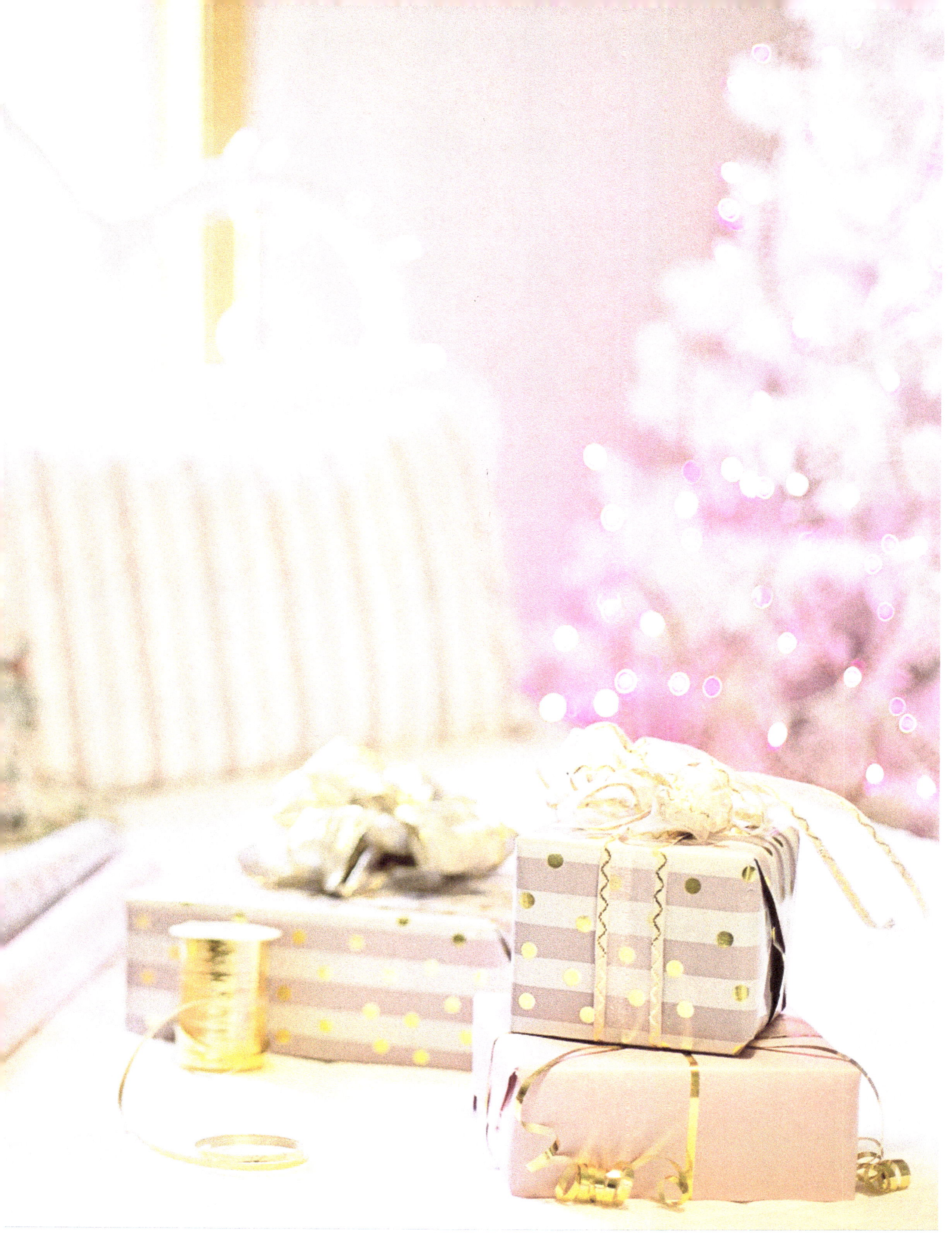

used. This way, the original designers' work is promoted and respected, while everyone can share their ideas.

## IMPORTED DESIGNS CAN NO LONGER BE SHARED

To prevent hacking, Cricut no longer supports sharing of user-uploaded images and designs. So if we have made a design in another program (Illustrator, Inkscape, Silhouette Studio, etc.), and then we have uploaded it to Design Space to use it, or we have downloaded an image from the internet and added it to our project, that project will not be able to be used by other users.

If we are on the computer, a message like this will appear: «It contains exclusive content,» and if we look at it from the App, it will tell us that it is not possible to open the project because it has invalid data.

In this way, Cricut Joy prevents piracy by preventing anyone from taking someone else's design and uploading it to their platform. However, the Cricut Community is a great way to share project ideas created with official Cricut designs. Everything stays at home.

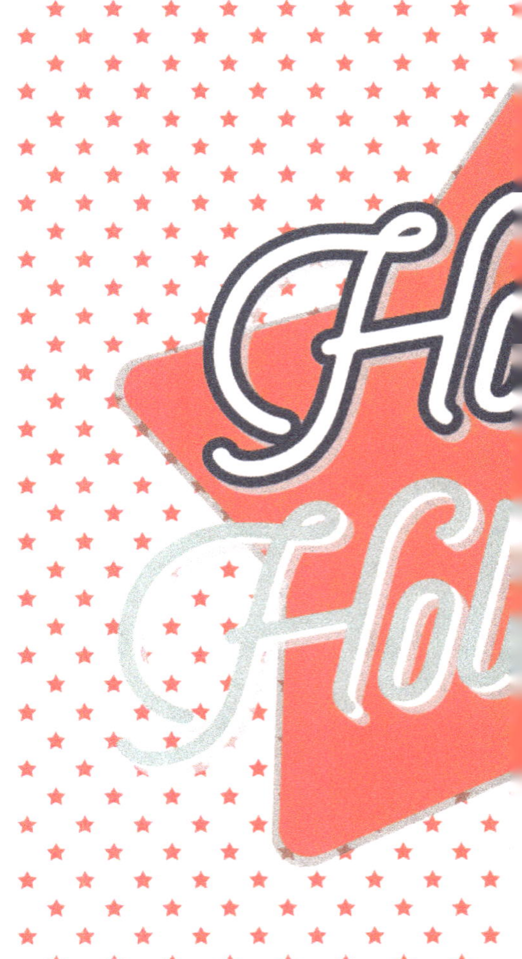

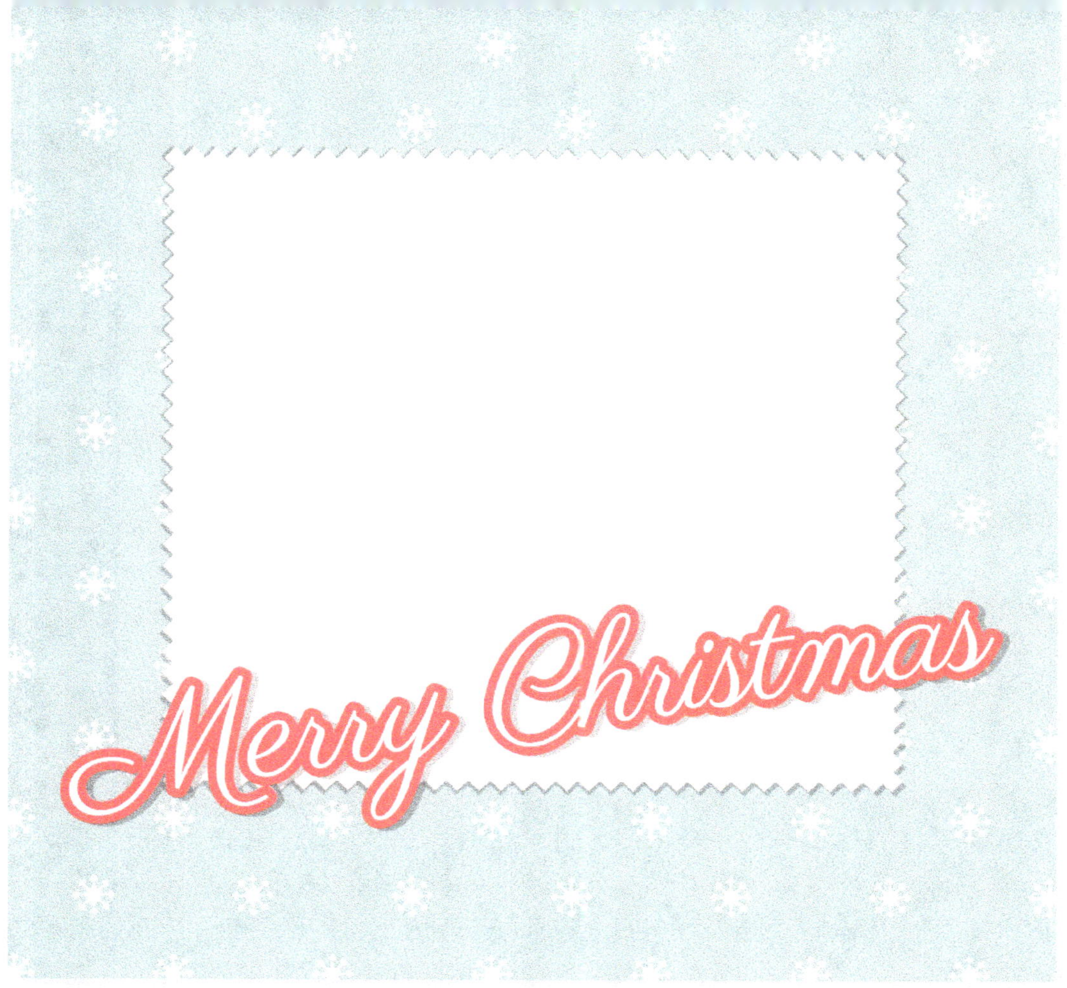
Merry Christmas
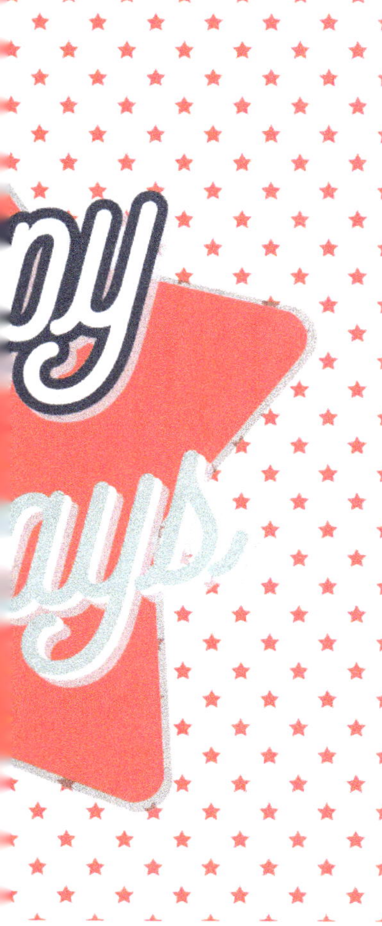

# Chapter 4
# Best Cricut Joy projects

## How to make Cricut Joy Labels

So, first off, you would have to decide on what project you want to work on. This is the fun part! As there are many things around your house, you can label making it look more beautiful! You could decide to make door labels for your kid at home; you could make labels on your drinking mugs, laptops, etc. Just let your imagination run wild!

Next, you need to decide on the size of the label. How large or small it will be. It depends on what exactly you want. You would need to get then the measurements of what you are working on. You need to measure the length and the width because you would need them for your design space.

You are choosing the right Vinyl for your project. This boils down to your preference-the type of vinyl you want to use and the color. When picking the kind of Vinyl material you wish to use, you should also consider if you're going to have the label permanent or temporary.

You can decide to get other surfaces such as

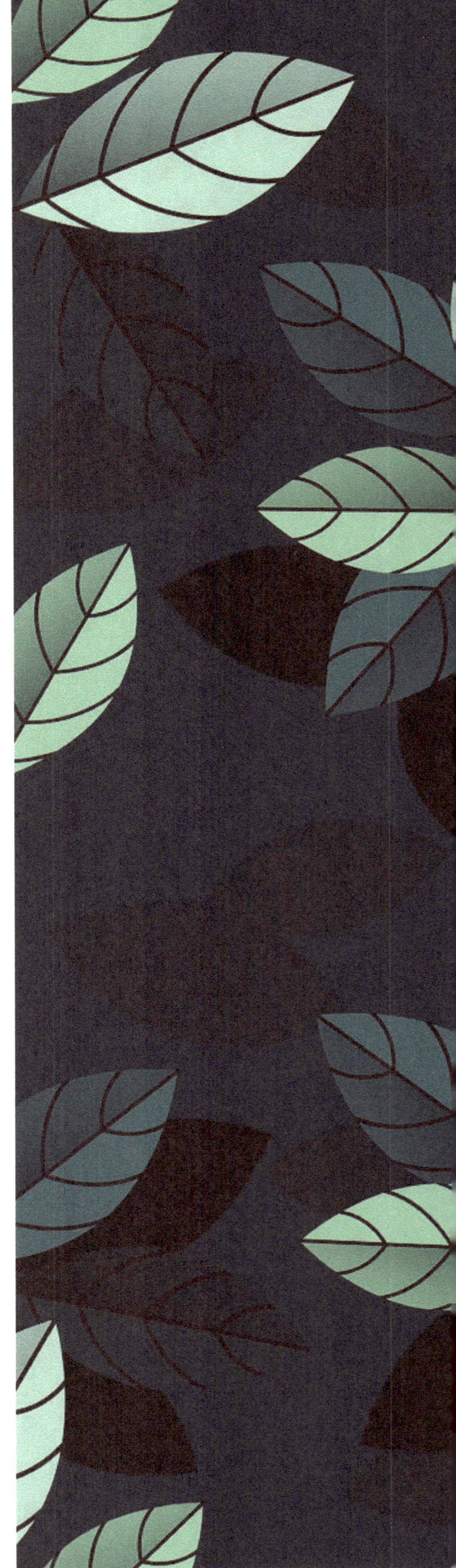

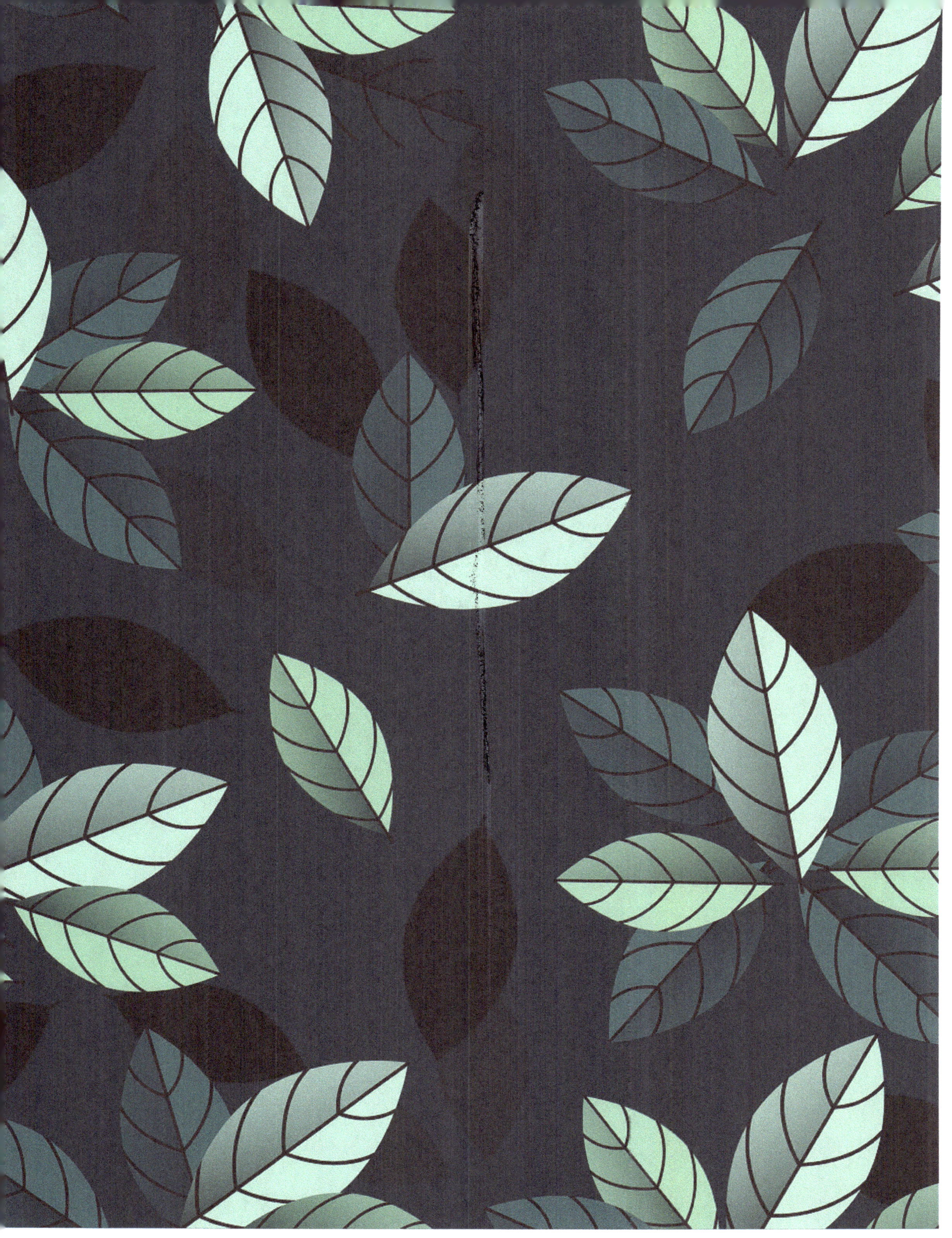

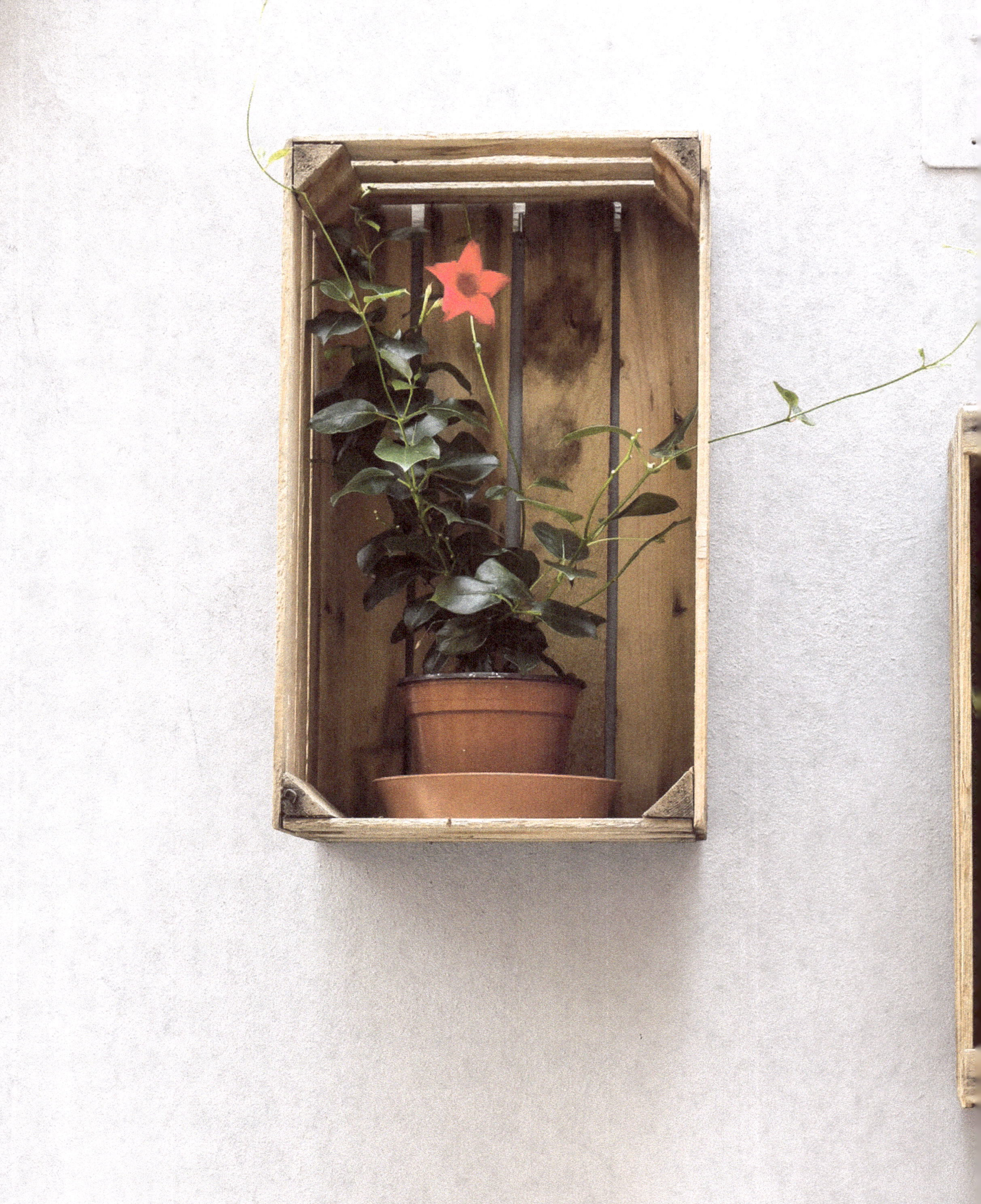

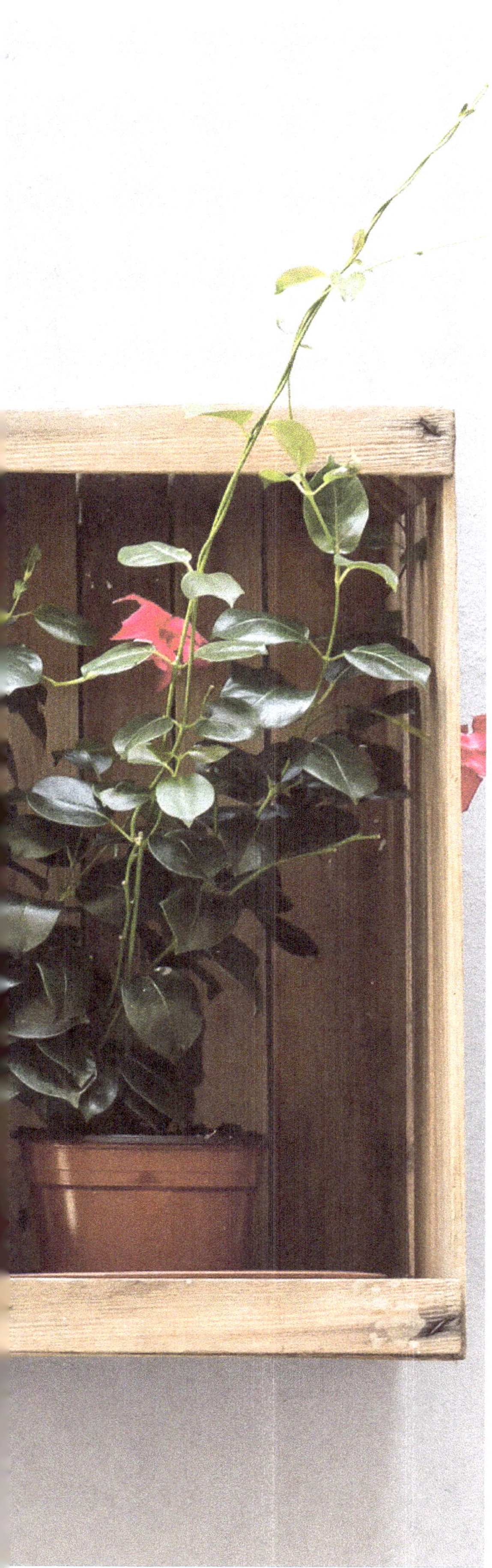

cards, paper, or even iron-or.

So, what's next to do?

Now you have to bring your design space know-ledge and skills to a test. Yes! You would have to design your label first on the design space software. You could get a lot of inspiration from their website; however, if it's merely a label that deals with just text, it's as easy as adding the text, change the fonts to your taste, and then adjust the size to fit the dimension you wanted. Tip: You can get a few numbers of fonts for free, and you can buy specific shapes and fonts on a one-off purchase. But, if you tend to use it a lot and optimize how much you spend. It saves you more money when you pay a monthly fee rather than paying every time you want to use a design. The perk is you get the first month free, so you get to see whether you use it enough before you go ahead to pay for the next month.

When you have finalized the design, you want to use, and you have clicked the "Make-it" on your design space software. You would then put your vinyl material into the Cricut Joy for cutting. When the Cricut Joy is done cutting, it would indicate that it is done on the design space software. Now that your design is on the vinyl. It's time to peel off the extra vinyl around your label. Peel it very slowly, and be careful when doing it not to peel off your main project with it.

Even after you have peeled off the extra vinyl around, there could still be some small pieces lying around. To get it off, we would use one of the Cricut Joy tools we talked about earlier. The

Weeder! Use the device and take off those bits. Now, pay attention, as this part could be a bit complicated. For letters and shapes of just one piece, you could easily just peel off the back and stick them carefully wherever you want them to be. However, if you are working with more than one piece, that is your label or design, and you have started to peel and stick them, it might be challenging to get each piece's exact distance apart. And if each element of the label is not looking equidistant and placed wrong, it might start to look messy.

Instead of trying to gamble the exact location of where a piece should be, what could you use to give you the same position?

The answer is a Transfer Tape! It is a sticky tape that allows you to pick up all your pieces at once from the label's backing. With the transfer tape, it is as easy as picking up your tags where they are with the transfer tape, and then together with the transfer tape, apply them on where you want the labels to be. After, you peel off the transfer tape leaving the title in place, and you are good to go! Your pieces are the same distance apart as they were in the design space. Not an inch away.

## Projects ideas

### VINYL STICKER CAR WINDOW

Materials and tools:

Cricut machine

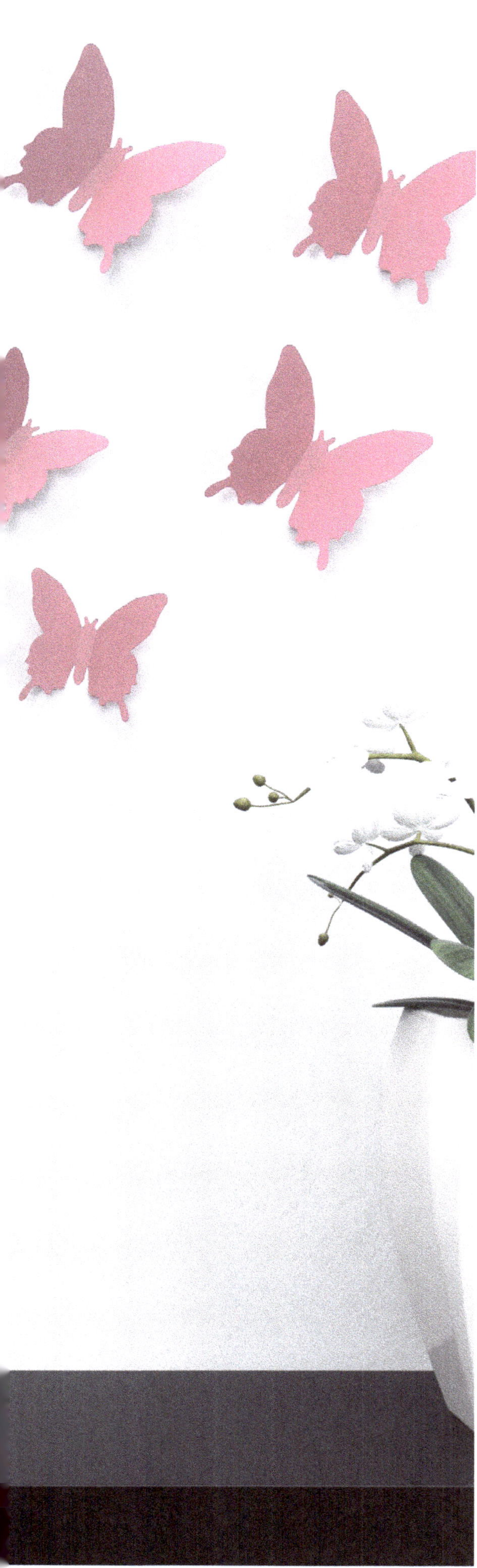

Premium outdoor glossy vinyl
Transfer tape
Scraper tool

Follow these steps to create:

Get and save the image you want to use online.
Log in to the Cricut design space and start a new project.
Click on the Upload icon and upload the saved image.
Click on the image and drag it to the next page, then select the image type.
Select the parts of the image you do not want as part of the final cut.
Select the image as a cute image. You will get to preview the picture as a cut image.
Approve the cut image. You would be redirected to the first upload screen.
Click on your just finished cut file, then highlight it and insert the image.
The image is added to your design space for size readjusting. The idea is ready to cut.
Cut the image and remove excessive vinyl after the image is cut.
Apply a layer of transfer tape to the top of the cut vinyl.
Clean the car window well with rubbing alcohol to remove all dirt.
Carefully peel away the paperback of the vinyl.
Apply the cut vinyl on the window. Start at one end and roll it down.
Go over the applied vinyl with a scraper tool to remove the air bubble underneath the vinyl.
Slowly peel away the transfer tape from the window.

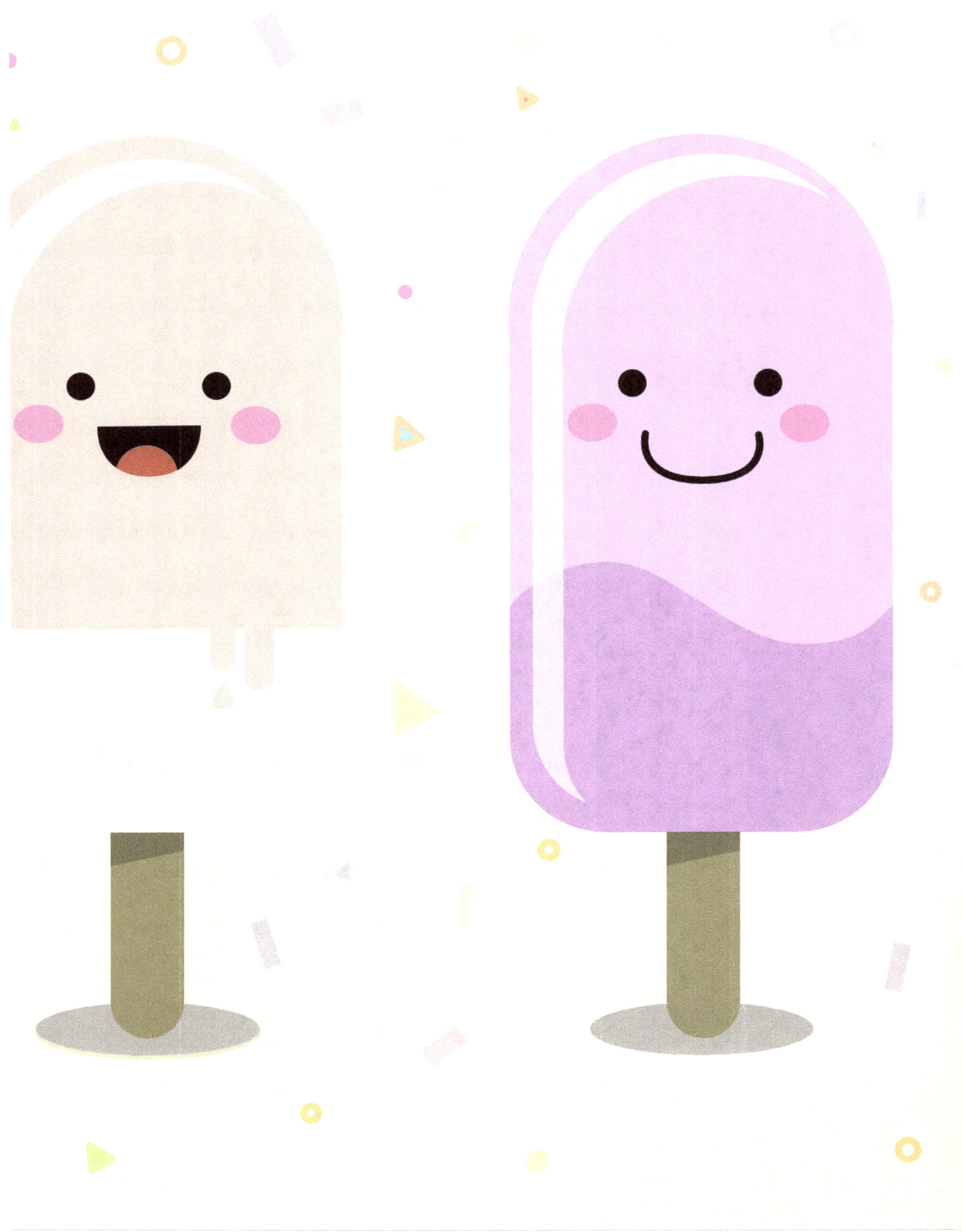

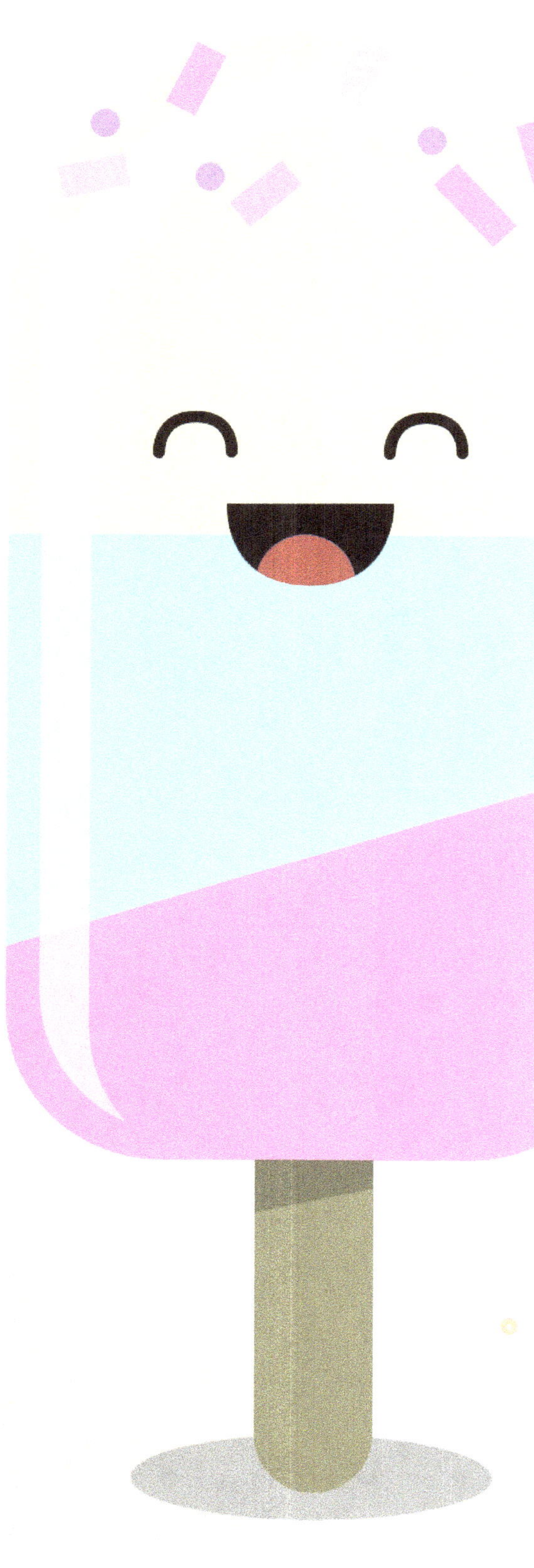

# ICE-CREAM STICKERS

Material and tools

Cricut machine
Printable sticker paper
Inkjet printer

Steps to making an ice-cream sticker:

Log in to the Cricut design spaces.
Start a new project and click on the Images on the screen's left side. Select the ice-cream image(s) you want.
Highlight the whole image and use the Flatten button to solidify the image as one whole piece.
Resize the image to the appropriate size you need. You realize this by clicking on the image then dragging the right side of the box to the extent you desire.
Click Save at the top left to save your project. Save it to be a print and cut image, after which you click the Make It button at the right hand of the screen.
Examine the result and click Cortinue if it's what you expected. This will lead you to print the design onto paper.
Adjust the dial on the Cricut machine to the required settings.
Place the sticker paper on the cutting mat.
Load the cutting mat into the machine and push it against the rollers.
Press the Load/Unload button and then the Go button to cut the stickers.
Sit back and let the machine print out your designed

sticker.

# FUN FOAM STAMPS

Materials and Tools

Craft Foam Sheets
Wooden blocks - small blocks, not larger than
4 inches
Glue
Cricut machine

Direction

Open your Design Space and go to Images. You
can search for the images through the library
by using specific words or browse through the
library to find the photos you like. You can choose letters as well if you would like to make
letter stamps. Numbers can be used as well. You
can use fun images of unicorns, hearts, stars, or
whichever shape or picture you find interesting.
Use the top editing panel to size the images for
your stamps. Images shouldn't be larger than 2
inches, but you can also make them larger or
smaller if you prefer. Make sure to size the ideas
to fit the wooden blocks.
Once you click on "Make it," make sure to set
the material to cutting foam as you will be
using foam sheets for your designs. You can cut
several images at once, while it is handy not to
have more than 6 x 2-inch images prepared
for cutting. Set your cutting mat and arrange
your foam material - you can use different co-



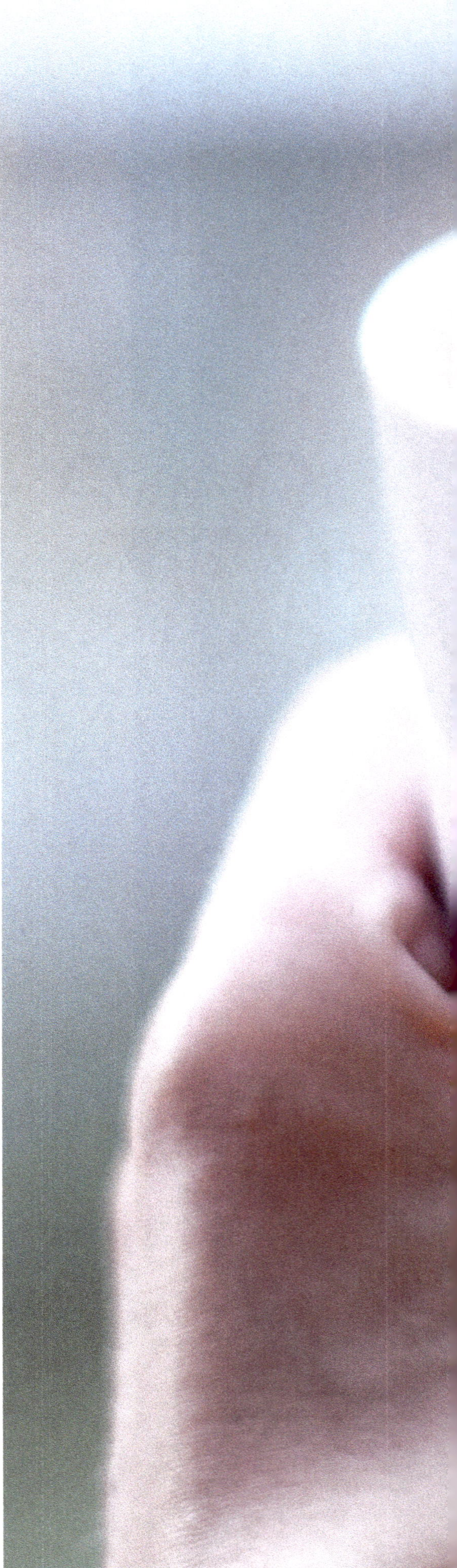

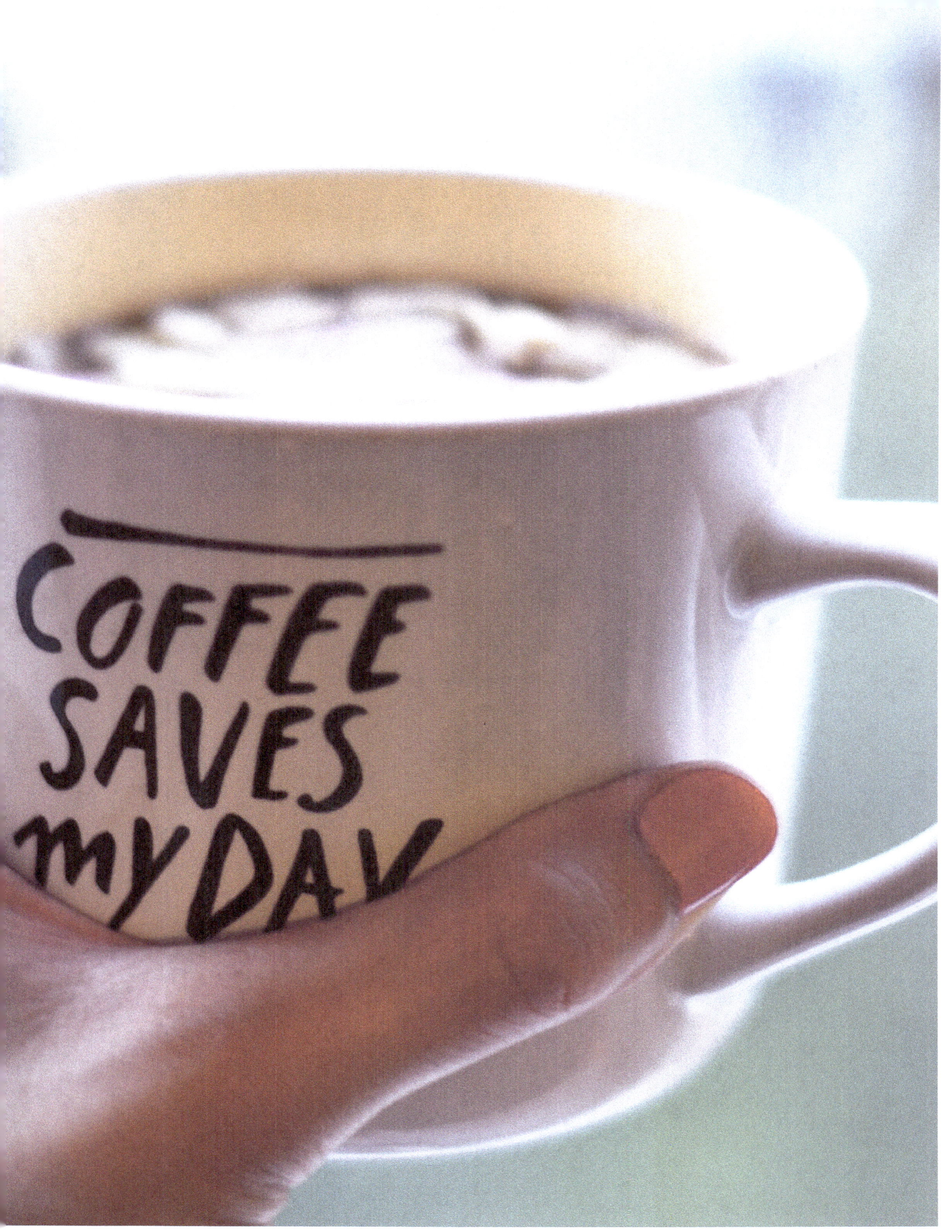

COFFEE
SAVES
MY DAY

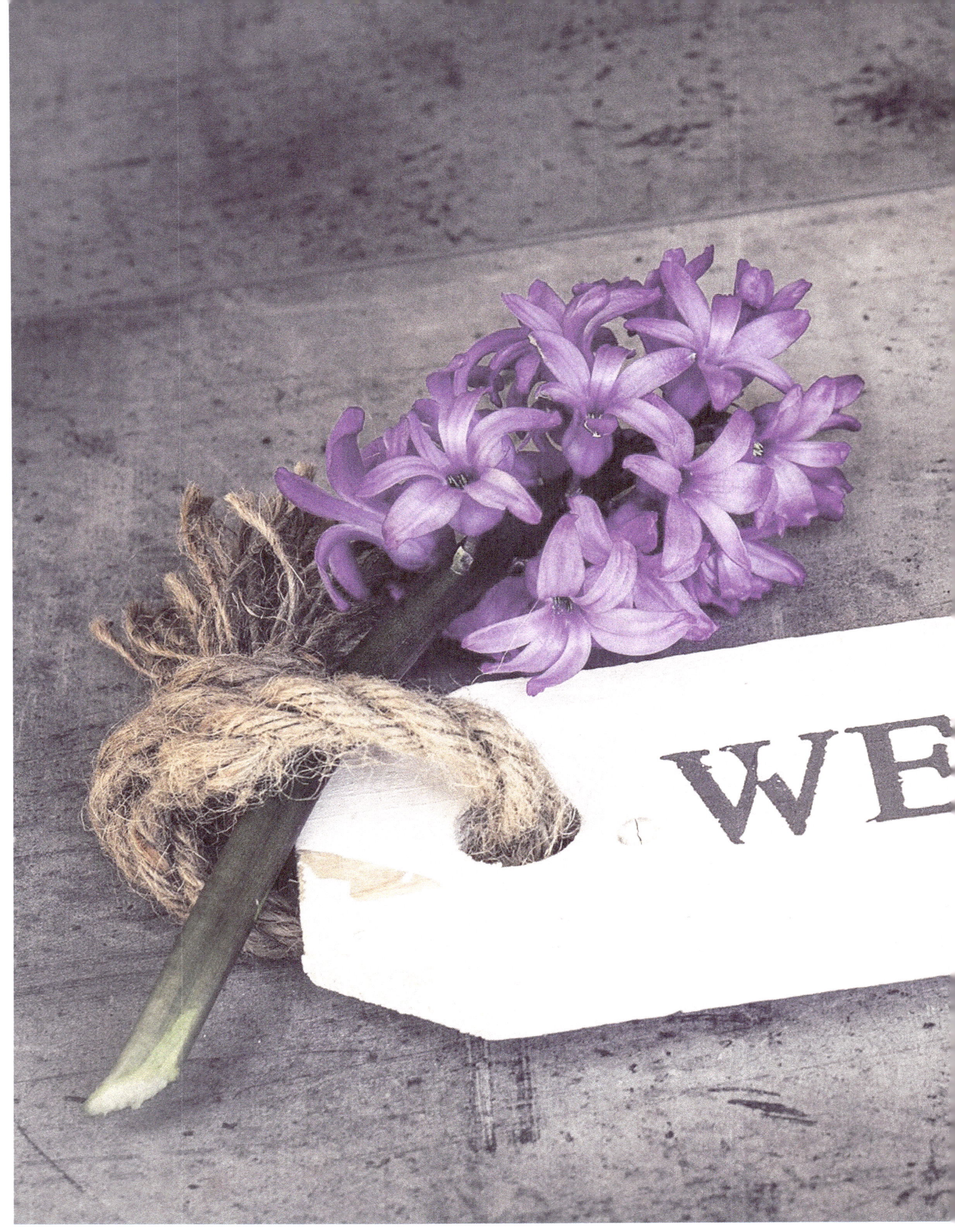
WE

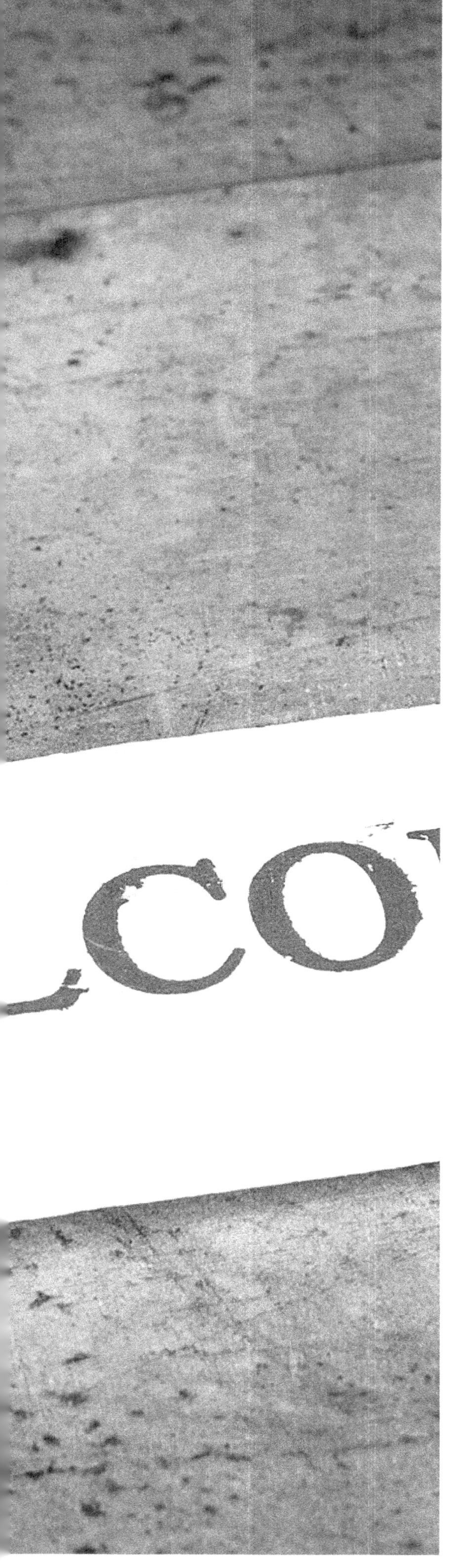

lors for different stamp images. Once you have set up everything, you can start cutting.

Once the images are cut out, you can start gluing them to the wooden blocks. It is best to let the dry glue overnight befcre you begin using stamps. You are all done and good to go!

## VINYL LABELS

Materials and Tools

Adhesive Vinyl
Transfer Tape
Glass jars
Cricut machine
SVG labels - alternatively, you can make your labels on Design Space using different fonts, shapes, and colors.
Spatula
Weeding tool

The idea is to have labe designs similar to this image. You can use different fonts and designs in case you are making your labels. If you are looking for the most comfortcble option, we recommend downloading and upload SVG labels to Design Space and use them for your jars. Let's see how we can make labeling easy and fun.

Direction

If you have decided to use a ready made designs for labels, upload your SVG file/files and start

editing. In case you are using ready-to-make designs, you will need to use the "eye" icon to hide
the labels you don't need in your first cutting or
don't need at all. By clicking on the "eye" icon on
the editing panel reserved for layers, you can
hide the labels you don't need at the moment.
Once you have chosen the brands you want to
cut, click "Ungroup."

Next is setting up specifications for cutting. Click
on the "Make it" button and choose vinyl for the
material used for cutting. Set your cutting mat,
then set the vinyl to prepare your Cricut. Once
all settings are in place, proceed to cut.

Your labels are cut out and ready, so it is time
for weeding. Use the weeding tool of your choice
to remove the excess vinyl from the brands.
Once you are done with weeding - make sure
you are careful not to cut through the vinyl, but
gently peel it off - you will cut out a piece of
transfer tape to match the size of the labels'
sheet. Peel off the paper from the back of the
video and place the tape's sticky side onto the
label sheet's front top. Make sure to press the
tape down.

Remove the vinyl from the cutting mat, then
cut out each label with the transfer tape still on
so you could have them individually applied on
the jars you wish to label with these super cool
designs.

For the finishing step, you will peel off the vinyl's
backing and press it down onto the jar while
trying to push all bubbles out and have the
labels applied correctly. Press hard to stick the
labels onto the jars. Remove the transfer tape
by peeling it off, and there you have your first
labeled jar!



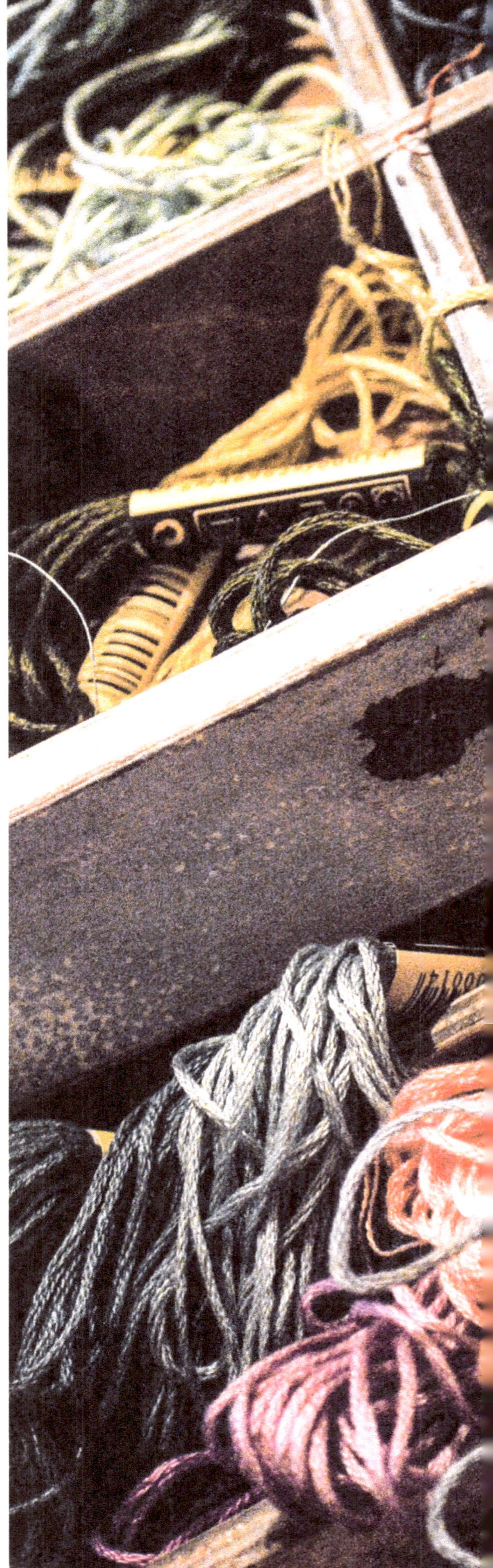

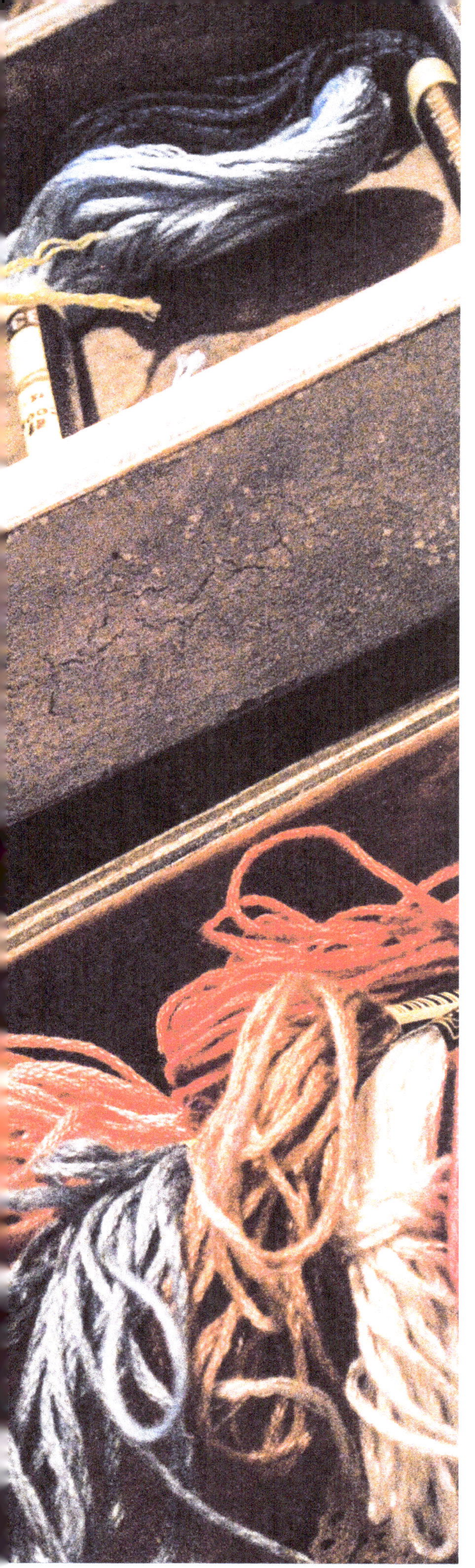

# CRICUT BOOKMARKER

Materials and Tools

Scrapbook
Scrapbook adhesive
6-inch twine
12-inch ribbon
Cricut machine

Direction

For the first step, you will find an SVG file you can use to make a bookmark, download it online, upload it to Design Space, or search for different designs in the library of images, paid and free. Another option is to create your design on Canvas and personalze your bookmark. Whatever option you decide to go for, you need to have your scrapbook paper cut in 6" x 2 1/4" and five 3/4" x 2". That means that you need to make a layer for your design according to these measures. You can always cut extra length if you would like the bookmarker to be smaller. You want to have two pieces of scrapbook so you can attach them once the parts are cut. That is how you will make one piece to be 6" x 2 1/4" and the other 5 3/4" x 2" on Design Space as well.

You can have different designs for each of the pieces and make sure that colors and designs are a perfect match when combined. You will also create a 1/4-inch hole on the top part of the bookmark pieces. You can choose "Shapes" and

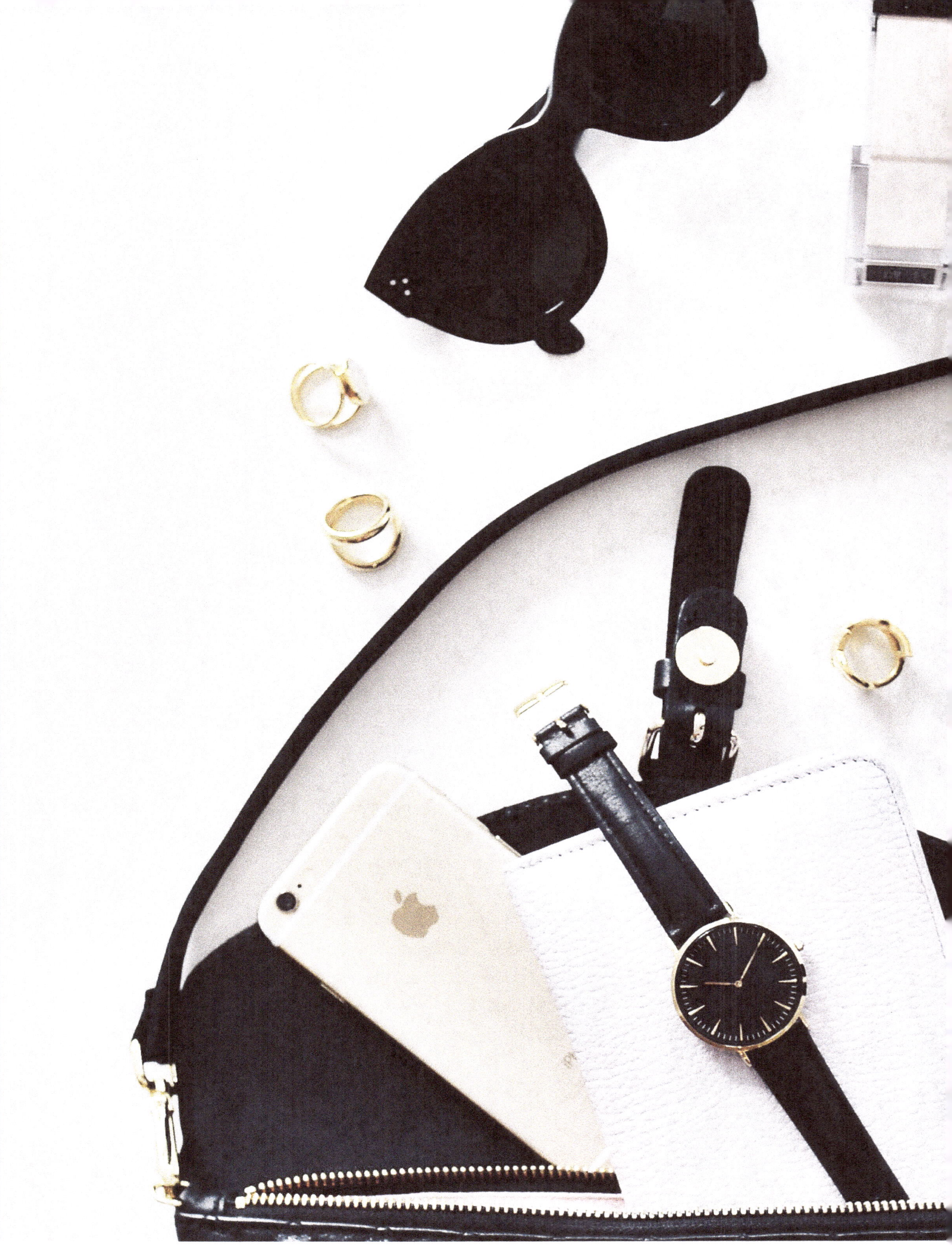

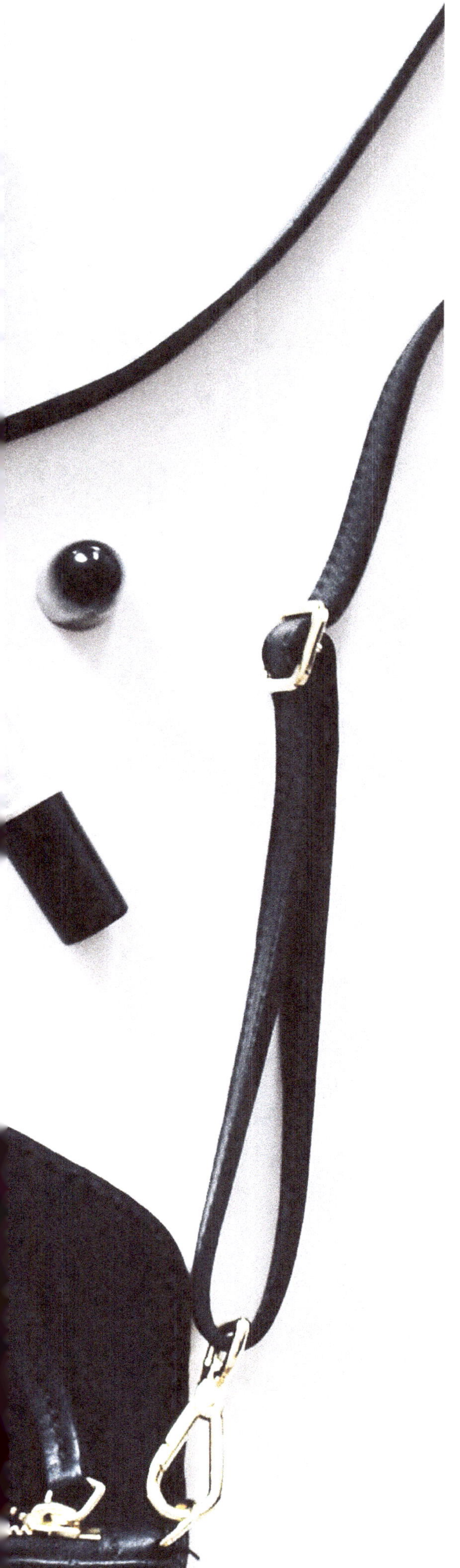

select the circle. And the process will appear on the canvas. Select the shape and click "Duplicate." Place each circle on the top of the bookmark pieces and adjust the size of the processes. Select the rings and click on "Weld" to cut out the holes. Alternatively, you can use a hole puncher as a tool instead. However, you can do all parts of the project with your Cricut machine.

Once you have the design ready, you can cut by clicking the "Make it" button. Make sure to select scrapbook paper as your material choice before cutting. Prepare the cutting mat and the material. Cut.

Once you are done with cutting, you will need to prepare your paper adhesive, twine, and ribbon. First, attach the two pieces of scrapbook paper with paper adhesive. Once the elements are fixated into one - make sure that the holes you've made on each piece are aligned - you can pull the ribbon through and even it by ends.

Use the twine to tie the ribbon by the edge of the bookmark. There you have it! Your personalized bookmark! You can use any design you want and try making different bookmarks with or without the ribbons and with additional details.

# PERSONALIZED PHONE CASE

Materials and Tools

Foil Adhesive Vinyl
Transfer tape
Clear phone case - more room for fun!
Weeding tool
Scissors or scalpel

Cricut machine - Cricut joy

Direction

As always, when starting fresh, click on "New Project" to open a blank canvas. You can make this project a breeze by clicking on "Templates." Here you can find templates for numerous different projects, which include phone cases as well. Choose the phone case template. Make sure to size the template layer to fit the size of the clear phone case you have prepared for the project. From there, you can start working on your design. You can add images of your choice and resize them as needed to make a phone case design.

Once your design is ready to go, you will click "Select All" then choose the "Attach" option. This will prepare the design for cutting as you need both the phone case rectangle layer cut out and the phone case designs.

If you are happy with your design, you can click on "Make it." Before proceeding with cutting, choose Foil Adhesive Vinyl as your material. Set up the cutting mat and prepare the material to start cutting.

Now that your design is cut out, it's time to use the weeding tool. Remove all excess vinyl from the design - in this case, extra material would be the background while your designs (butterflies, for example) should remain intact. Next, attach the transfer tape to the vinyl and remove the backing paper. Attach the vinyl to the phone case with the transfer tape. You will use your

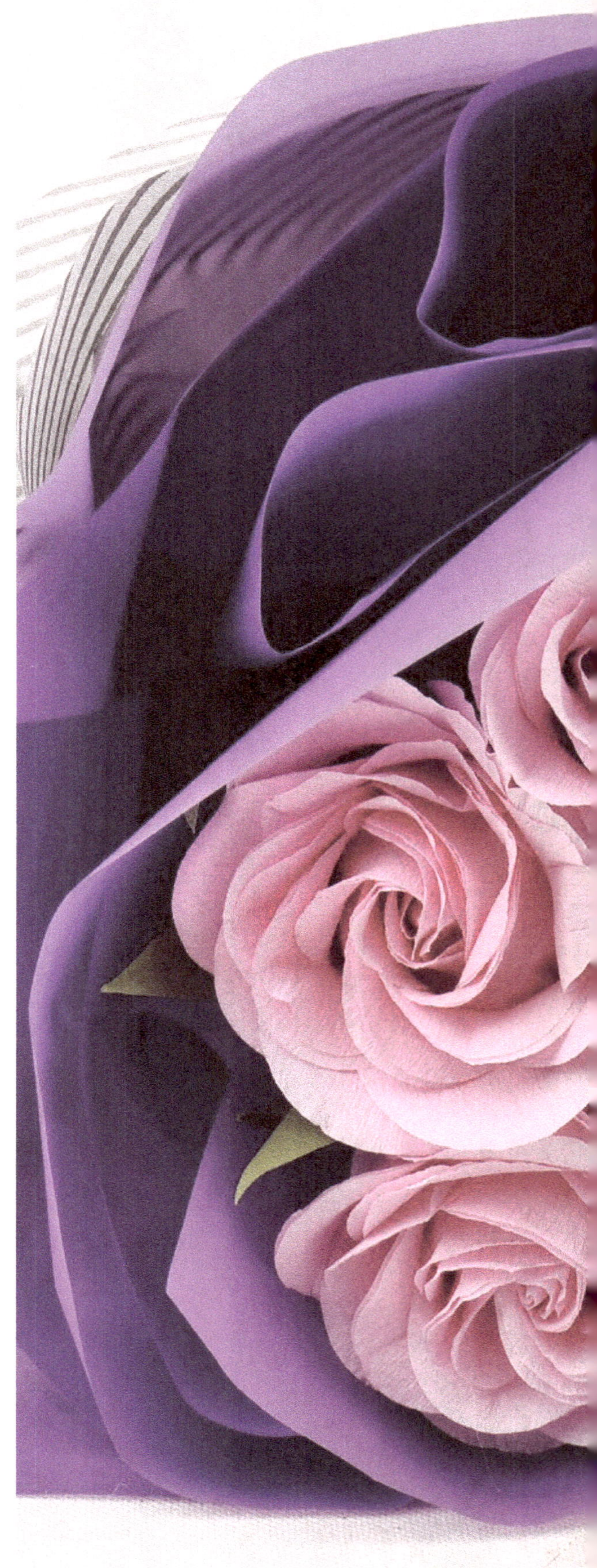

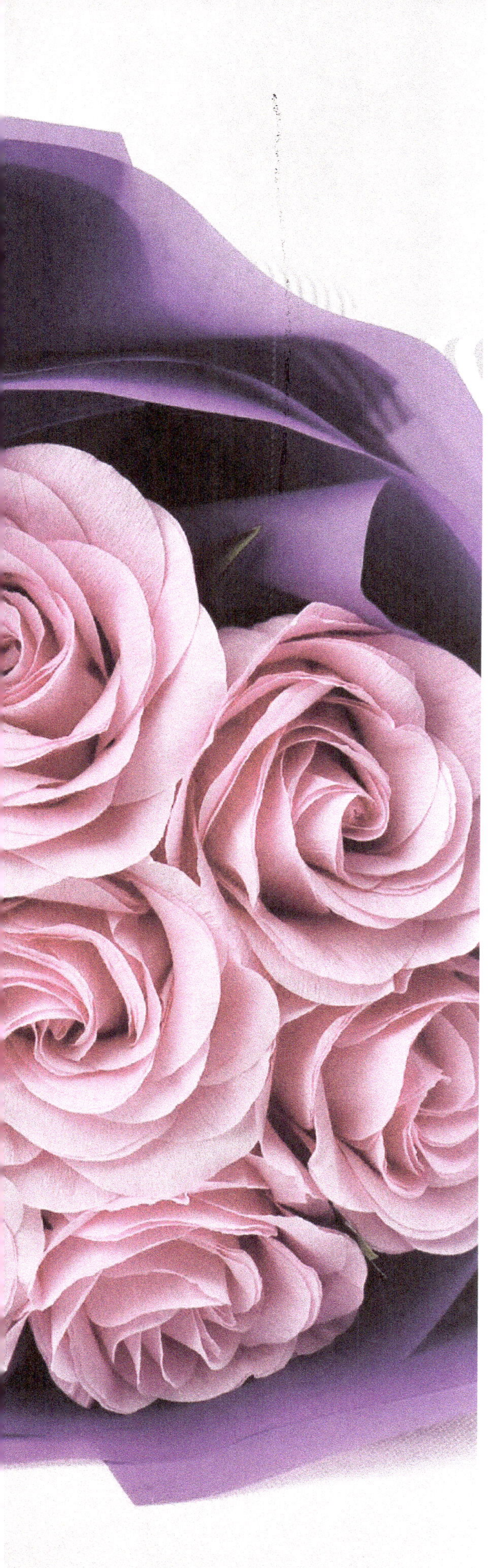

scissors or a scalpel to remove the vinyl's spare part once attached to the phone case - remove those parts that don't fit the phone case design. For instance, you will need to remove the vinyl piece covering the camera slot on the phone case. Remove the tape, and voila! You have your personalized phone case. You can make as many designs as you like using these guidelines.

# PAPER DAISIES

Materials and Tools

Cardstock
Glue
Quilling tool
Cricut machine

Direction

Once you click on "New Project," you can upload a design to the Design Space or download a daisy design online and use it after uploading it to the software. You can also make your designs, although this option will take more time and planning as you will be later quilling these patterns - that means that you need to make sure that the design you create on the Canvas can be later folded quilted into a lovely paper daisy. You want your design to look like so, while you can choose any color you desire or add multiple colors for multiple cardstock pieces and make colorful daisies:

As you can notice, you will need a spiral design

with petals for making a paper daisy. You can resize your spiral designs to match the arrangement of smaller daisies and follow your paper decorations. In case you wish to have colorful daisies, you can mix and check different sets of daisy designs once you cut them in different cardstock colors. For this, you will make fair use of scissors and glue - preferably; you will be using a glue gun to complete the task more comfortably and faster.

Once your design is ready, you will click on "Make it" as you specify your materials in Design Space to cardstock. Prepare your cutting mat and cardstock in the chosen color (colors), then proceed to cut.

When the spiral with the petals is cut out, you can begin quilting. Start from the inner part of the circle. Take a quilling tool and start rolling the spiral inwards until you get a lovely blooming daisy. Ensure that all the petals are faced outwards from the center of the daisy and glue the bottom of the cardstock design to keep the petals tightly arranged. Your first paper, daisy, is done and ready! You can repeat the process for more colorful daisies and combine more colors to create colorful designs.

# JAR LUMINARIES

Materials and Tools

Black vinyl
Acrylic sealer - clear
Acrylic paint
Painting brush

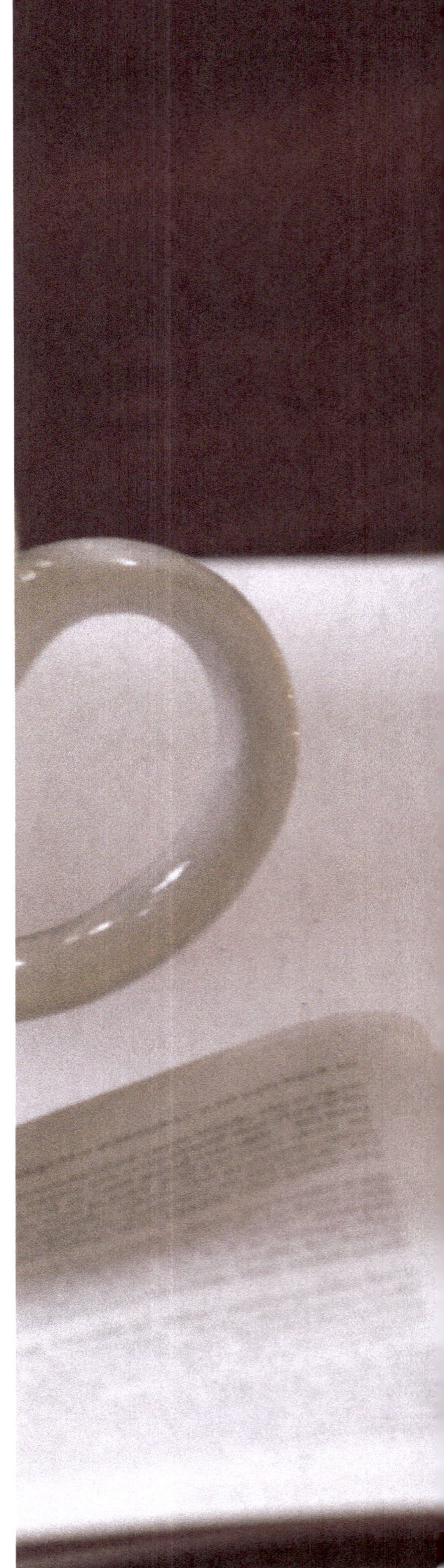

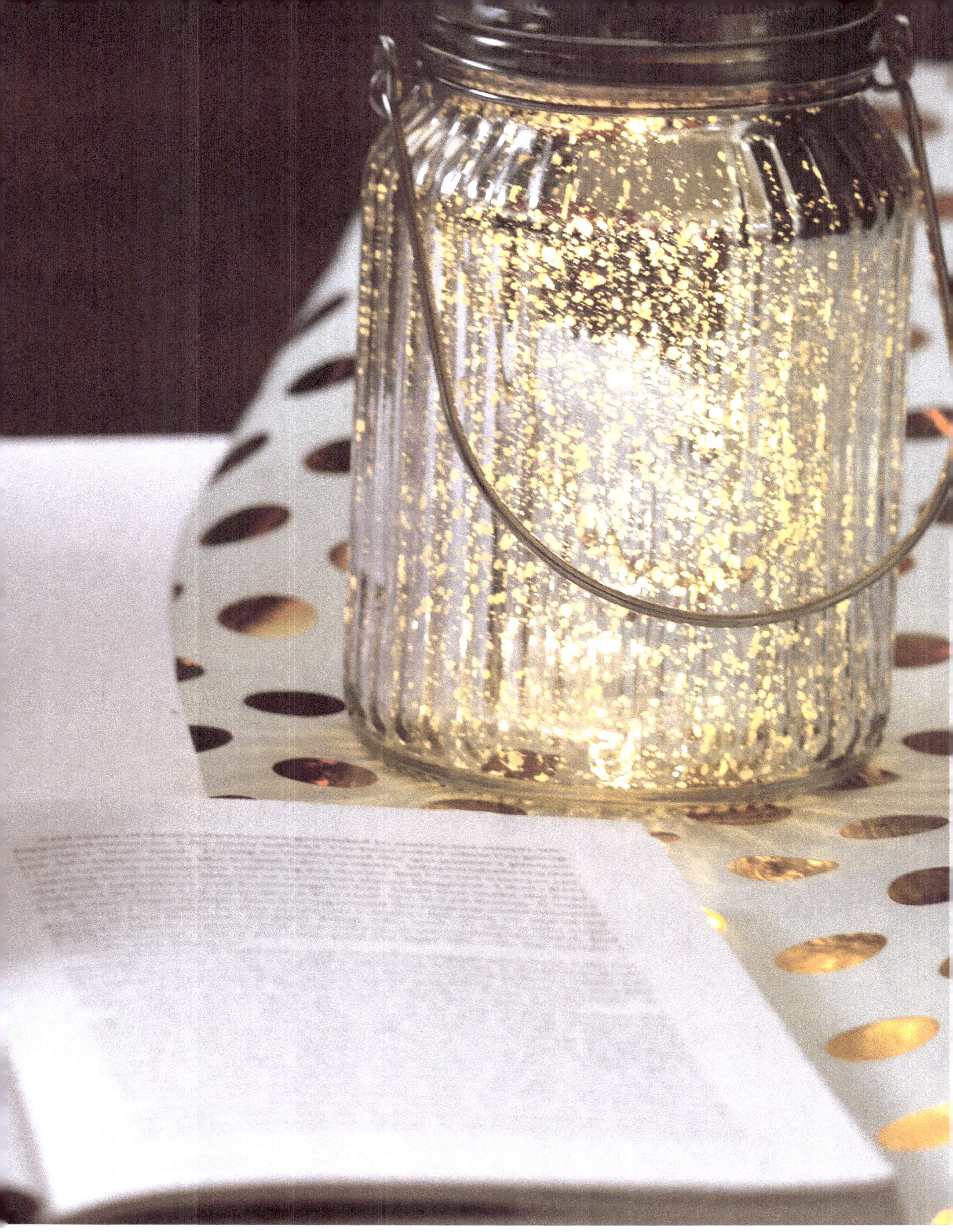

Cricut machine

Direction

Pick the color of your acrylic paint, get your paintbrush and start painting the jar. You will do this first as you need to leave the paint to dry for a while before applying the vinyl onto the jar. Next, you will open Design Space and click on "New Project." You can either upload a design in the SVG file, find a suitable image in the library of images in the Design Space. You can also create (draw) your plan and send it to cut. First off, you will need to select the image you wish to use, then measure your jar to pick the size of your design. Size the design by directly selecting the procedure or by typing specific measures in the top editing panel of the Design Space.
Send the design to cut by clicking on "Make it" - specify the material you wish to use - in this case, vinyl - then proceed to cut. Make sure that your cutting mat is in place together with the material you plan to use.
Once the design is fixated, apply the acrylic sealer to protect the design alongside the paint. You can use a tealight candle or LED lights for your luminaires. Enjoy the sparkles and make more jars whenever you feel like so.

# PERSONALIZED PILLOWCASE

Materials and Tools

Iron-on Vinyl

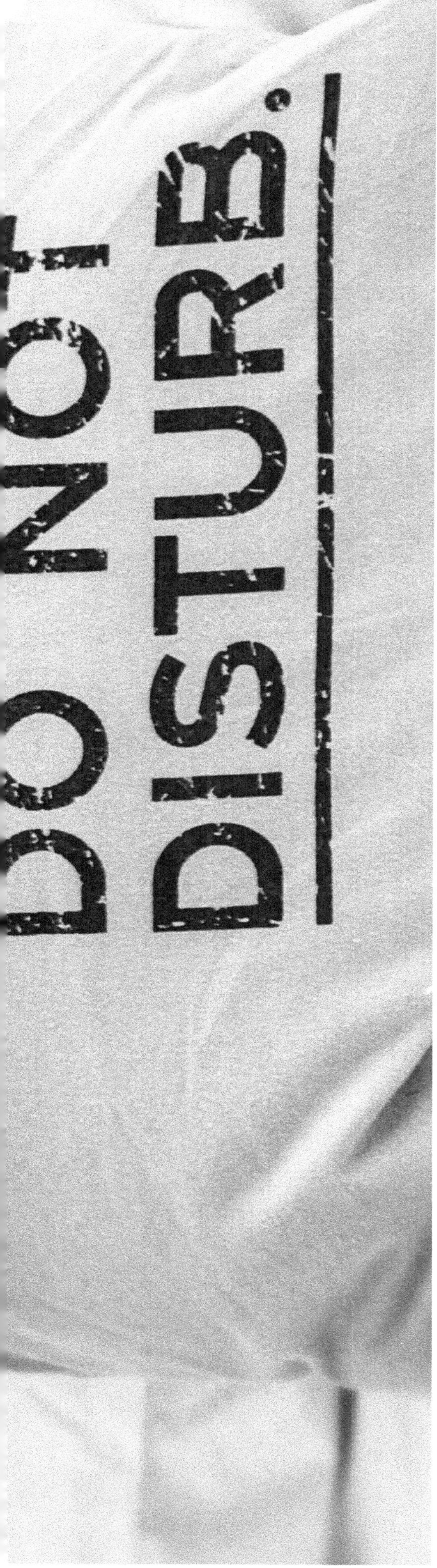


Pillowcase
Weeding tool
Cricut Machine
Easy Press or iron

Direction

Upload your preferred design or choose one from the Design Space image library. You can also make your own design. Make sure to adjust the size of the image to the size of the pillow - you don't want the image to be too small, but you don't also want it to go over the entire surface of the pillow.

You can also create a mock-up statement or a witty citation by using a font of your choice. When your design is ready, you can proceed to "Make it" - there; you will specify iron-on vinyl as your material of choice. Make sure to use "Mirror" on your design as you will be attaching the image to the pillow. Before you start cutting the image with the machine, set up your cutting mat and arrange the material. Proceed to cut.

Your design is cut, and now it's the time for weeding. Take your wedding tool and start removing all the excess vinyl from your design until only the image you want or the pillow is left. Remove all vinyl scraps from the working surface and prepare your Easy Press or regular iron. Heat your Easy Press - you can set the timer on.

The heating up will take 5 seconds. Afterward, you will heat the pillow surface for 30 seconds before attaching the design to the pillow. Place the vinyl on the pillow where you want the image to be, then use the Press again. Make sure to apply mild pressure onto the Press and hold for 15 seconds. Let the vinyl piece cool a bit before removing it from the pillow and revealing your new design. At this moment, the vinyl is too hot so that you can burn your fingers. Once the vinyl piece is cool or warm, you can remove it and enjoy your design.

# FUN STATEMENT SIGN

Materials and Tools

Black vinyl
Transfer paint
Wooden pieces:
1×12 cut to 9 inches
(2) 12-inch trim pieces cut from a 1×2 with 45° angles on each end
(2) Ten ½-inch trim pieces cut from a 1×2 with 45° tips on each end
Nails for the frame
Hammer
Sandpaper
Black paint
White paint
Weeding tool
Cricut machine

Direction

Before you start the Design Space, you will need

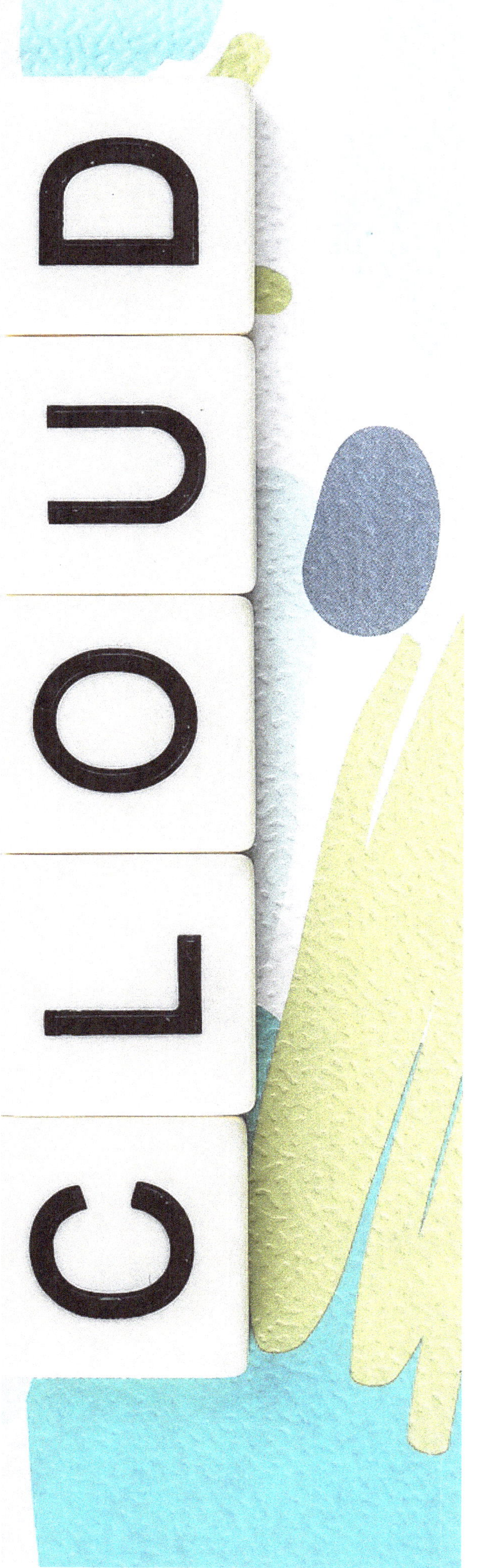


to take care of the wooden piece and the frame. In case you already have a blank framed sign, you can skip this process and move forward with designing. Alternatively, you will want to use sandpaper on the wooden pieces and sand them a bit before painting.

The black paint is for the frame pieces, and the white paint is for the wooden board that will be the surface for your Cricut design. Leave the wooden pieces to dry and move forward to working in Design Space.

Pick an image in the Design Space from the Image library or make your design. You can use any style or font you like for letters if you are making a statement design. The library has a wide offer of images and designs, so you will probably find a perfect match for your design there.

Once your design is ready, make sure to set the size to fit the wooden board you have painted white. Proceed to cut by clicking on "Make it" and select your material preferences to vinyl. Once everything looks good and ready to go, you can start cutting with your Cricut machine.

Once the paint on the wooden pieces is dry, you can use the hammer to nail the frame pieces together and frame the white wooden work. In the meantime, you can start weeding the vinyl parts you don't need on your design.

Do not cut. Try your vinyl but peel it off from one angle with your weeding tool and try to peel it off in entirety with your finger carefully. You can use the weeding tool as well if you feel

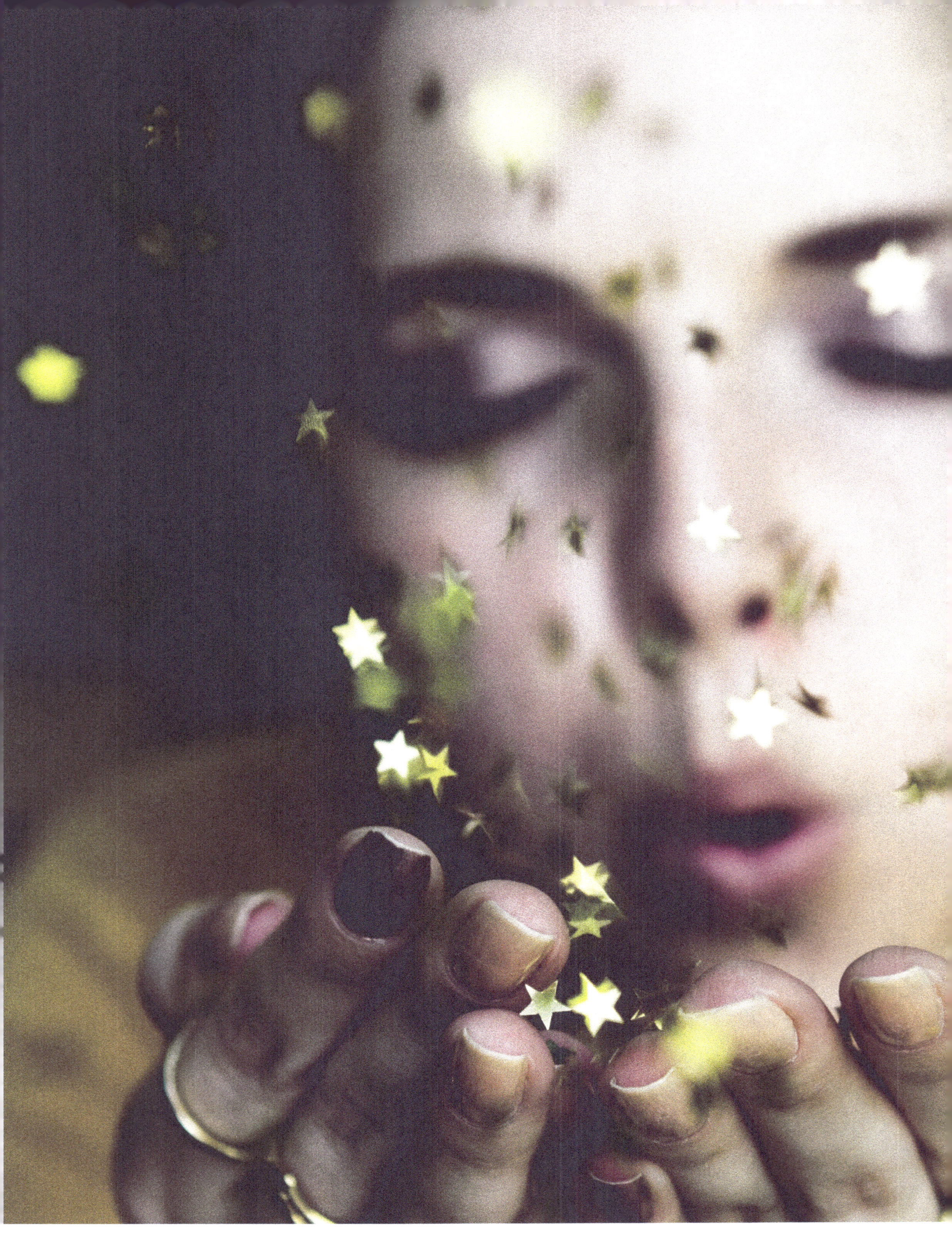

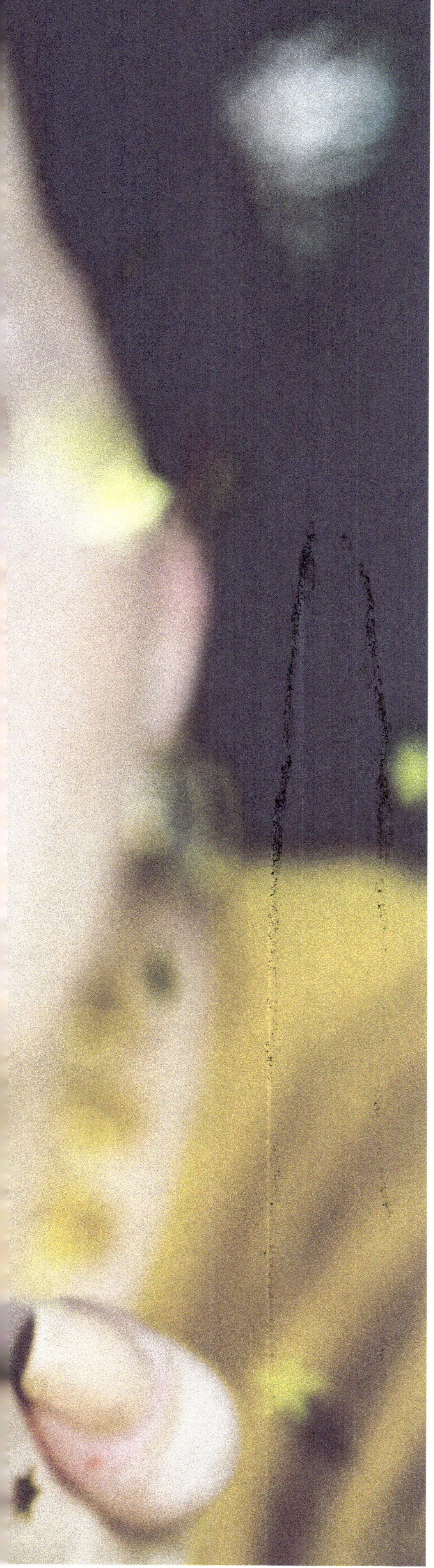

more comfortable with that. Next, you will apply the transfer tape to your clean design. Cut out the video to fit the sign's surface, then use the tape with the vinyl piece. Remove the transfer tape after carefully applying it, and you have your wooden sign ready!

## PARTY POPPERS

Materials and Tools

Cardstock - 12" x 12"
Ribbon
Treats and trinkets to use as a surprise for your party poppers - make sure not to use items larger than 3 inches
Cracker snaps and glue for gluing the pictures are optional - in case you want to have that cracking sound when popping the party poppers, you can find these online in bundles Cricut machine

Direction

You first want to download patterns for party poppers, or you can make your design. In case you decide to find the way and download it, you need to upload it in the form of an SVG file when starting a new project in Design Space. Your design is supposed to look like so on the Canvas:
As you may notice, the design is not particularly difficult to make. However, it would help if you

made sure that two-party poppers can fit the cardstock in the given size. This design represents the cut for two-party poppers.

Make sure to use "Attach" for each piece of design. Select the first three layers and attach them. Do the same thing for the second row of layers so these parts would be cut together as a whole. Once your design is ready, make sure to select cardstock for your material. Arrange the cutting mat and the cardstock piece, then "Make it" and cut the design.

Once the party popper designs are cut out, prepare two ribbon pieces for each and roll the cardstock designs in tubes by length. In case you are using cracker snaps, glue them on the inside lengthwise instead of in the middle before moving the cardstock.

Tie one end of the tube with a ribbon, then fill the box with surprise treats and trinkets. Tie the remaining end of the tube, and you have your first party popper.

## CRICUT GIFT BOXES

Materials and Tools

Glitter cardstock or another type of cardstock
Glue
Scoring Wheel
Cricut machine

Direction

You will start by designing your box pattern or by uploading SVG files for box patterns - there

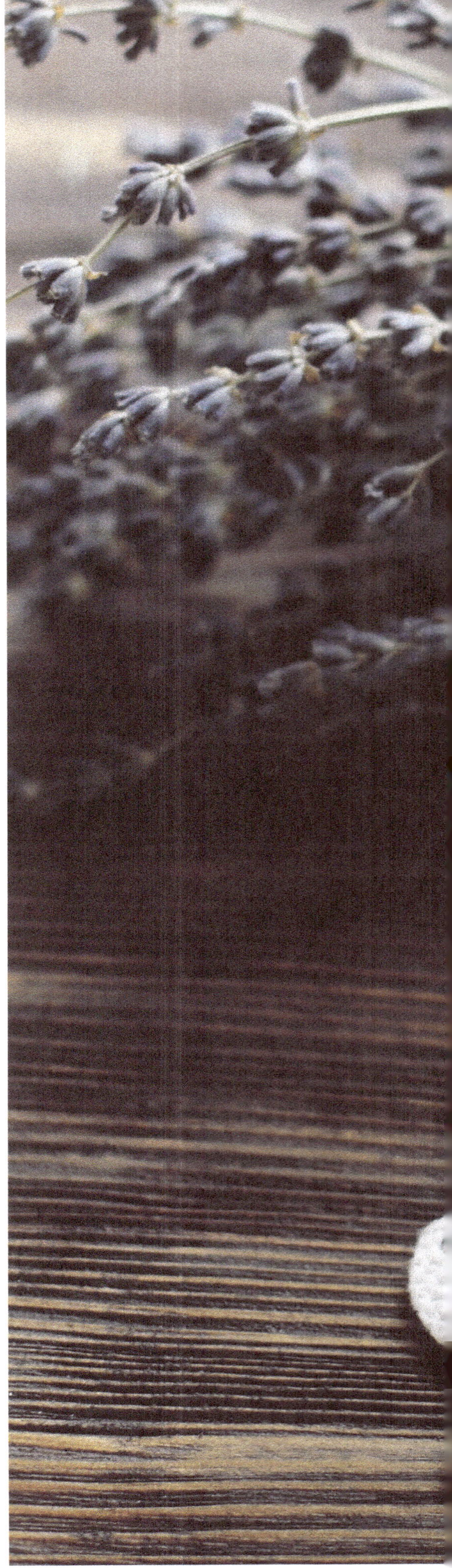

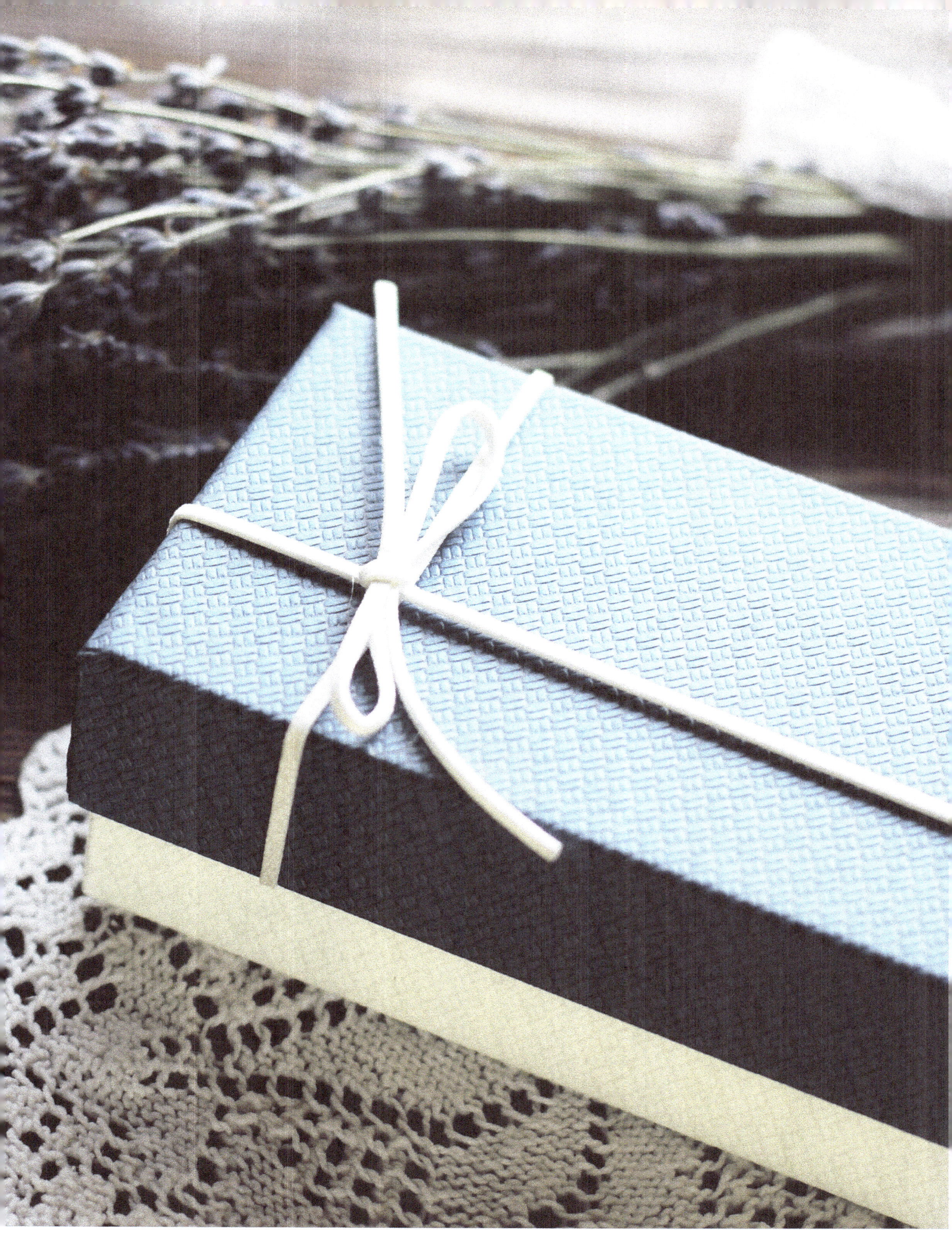

are numerous designs for boxes found online, while you can also make your designs if you are good with creating ways that should be later assembled.

You can use patterns similar to this made for this pillow style box:

Or use some similar to these designs:

Once you access your Design Space, click on "New Project" and upload the patterns you have found and downloaded. Alternatively, start making your patterns for boxes. You can withdraw from the pillowcase box as perhaps the simplest to make for a beginner.

Size your patterns to fit the box's intended size by using the top editing panel in Design Space. In case you are making more than a single package (perhaps you are making smaller gift boxes), make sure to press "Ungroup" to separate designs that should be cut and used separately for assembling.

Make sure to change the Line type to "Score" for parts of the design that should be folded before sending your design to cut. When you are finished scoring the lines that need to be folded, select the entire design and click on "Attach", finish the sizing if needed from this point, and then click on "Make it."

Choose cardstock as your preferred material when specifying cutting settings under "Make it." Once you have prepared the material and the cutting mat, you can proceed to cut. After this step, you will assemble your box/boxes.

In case you have chosen light materials such as paper or regular cardstock, you won't need to glue the box to keep the parts together. However, if you are using glitter cardstock and similar materials, you will need to secure the details of the box with glue - except the part that is supposed to seal (close) the box.

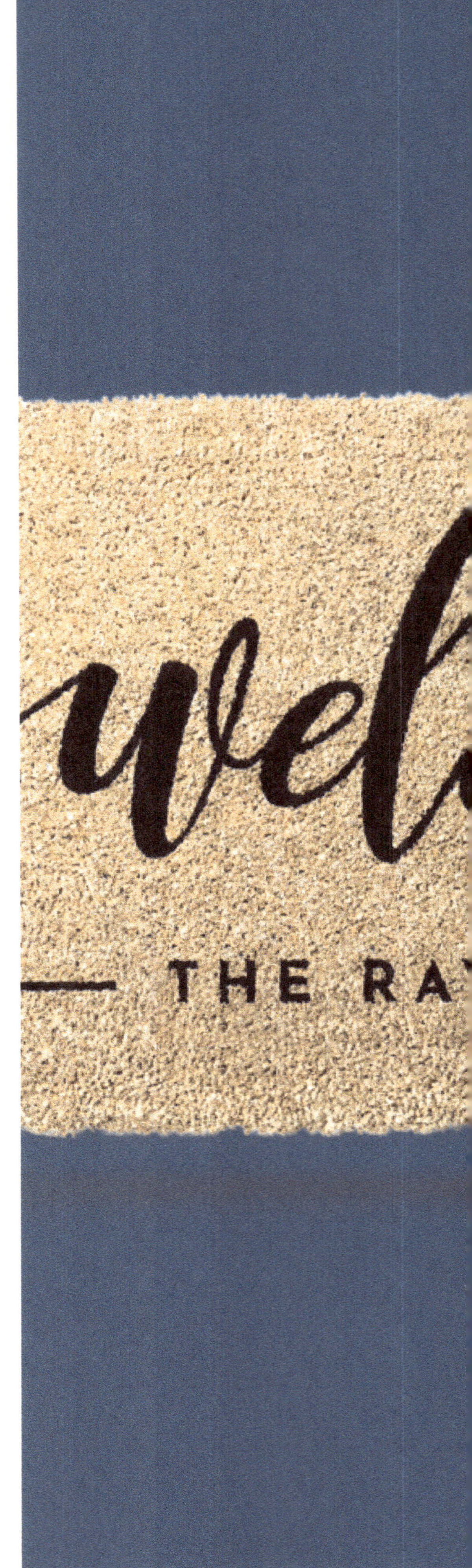

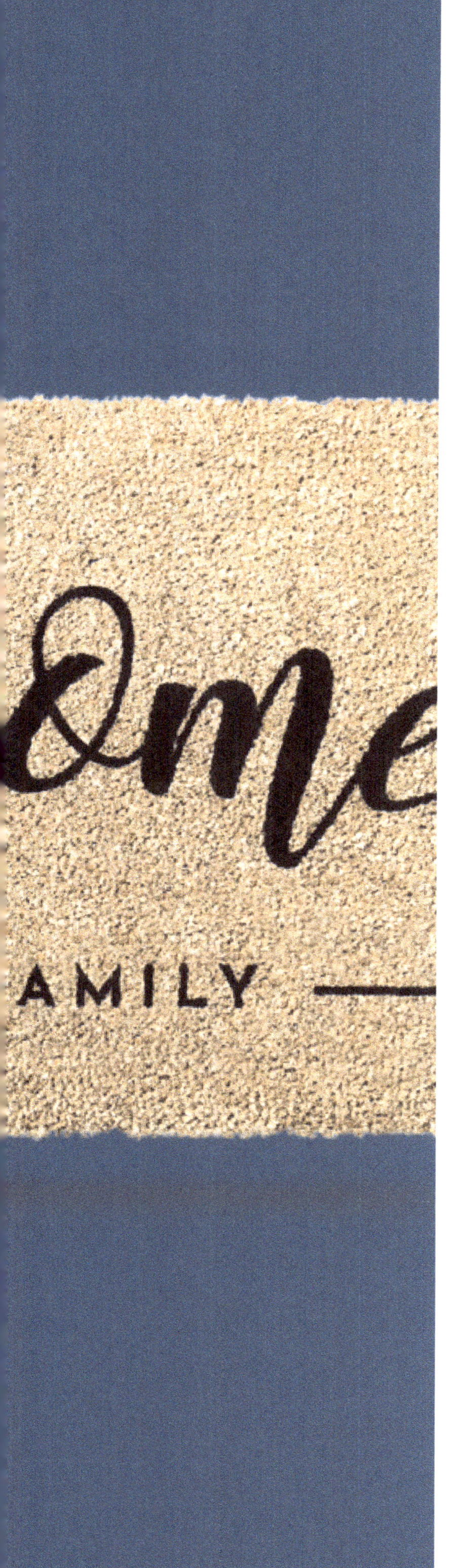


Start assembling your box and glue the parts that need to be secured as you go. The best is to use tacky glue or glue gun to make things faster and more efficient. And your box is ready!

## PERSONALIZED DOORMAT

Materials and Tools

Heavy cardstock
Doormat - plain
Stencil brush
Tape
Fabric paint
Cricut machine
Gloves are recommended since you will be using fabric paint

Direction

What is essential for you to make for this project is the pattern for your doormat - you can use a cute design or go for a witty statement written in a bold and exciting font. You can also download the SVG file with an already-ready design. In case you are uploading the SVG file, you will have fewer steps to complete as you will be able to proceed to cut in only a couple of steps.
In case you are starting from scratch, make sure to create a base element for your design - this would be a layer on which you will place your statement or another cool design. You can choose any font you like, and in case you are searching for

an interesting image, you can always browse through the image
library. Once you have the design ready, you need to select the layers and click on "Weed." You want to cut and weed the image, then remove the negative part - the negative aspect would be the letters inside your design. You will need the letters to be cut out, so you could make a paint pattern for the doormat. Once your design is ready and you are happy with the outcome, you can click on the "Make it" button to send your invention to cut.

Make sure to prepare the material and your mat and set the cutting preferences to heavy cardstock. You will use heavy cardstock as your stencil. When the cutting is done, take the tape, the paint, and the brush alongside your pattern, and let's move onto the finishing step.

For the final step, you will carefully glue the edges of the pattern with tape so you can fixate it to the doormat.

Take the stencil brush and use it to apply paint over the pattern. Careful not to paint outside the edges of the pattern. Paint over the letters. Let the doormat dry, remove the pattern, and wish your visitors a warm welcome with a personalized doormat.

## VINYL WALL DECALS

Materials and tools

Adhesive vinyl
Cricut machine
Weeding tool

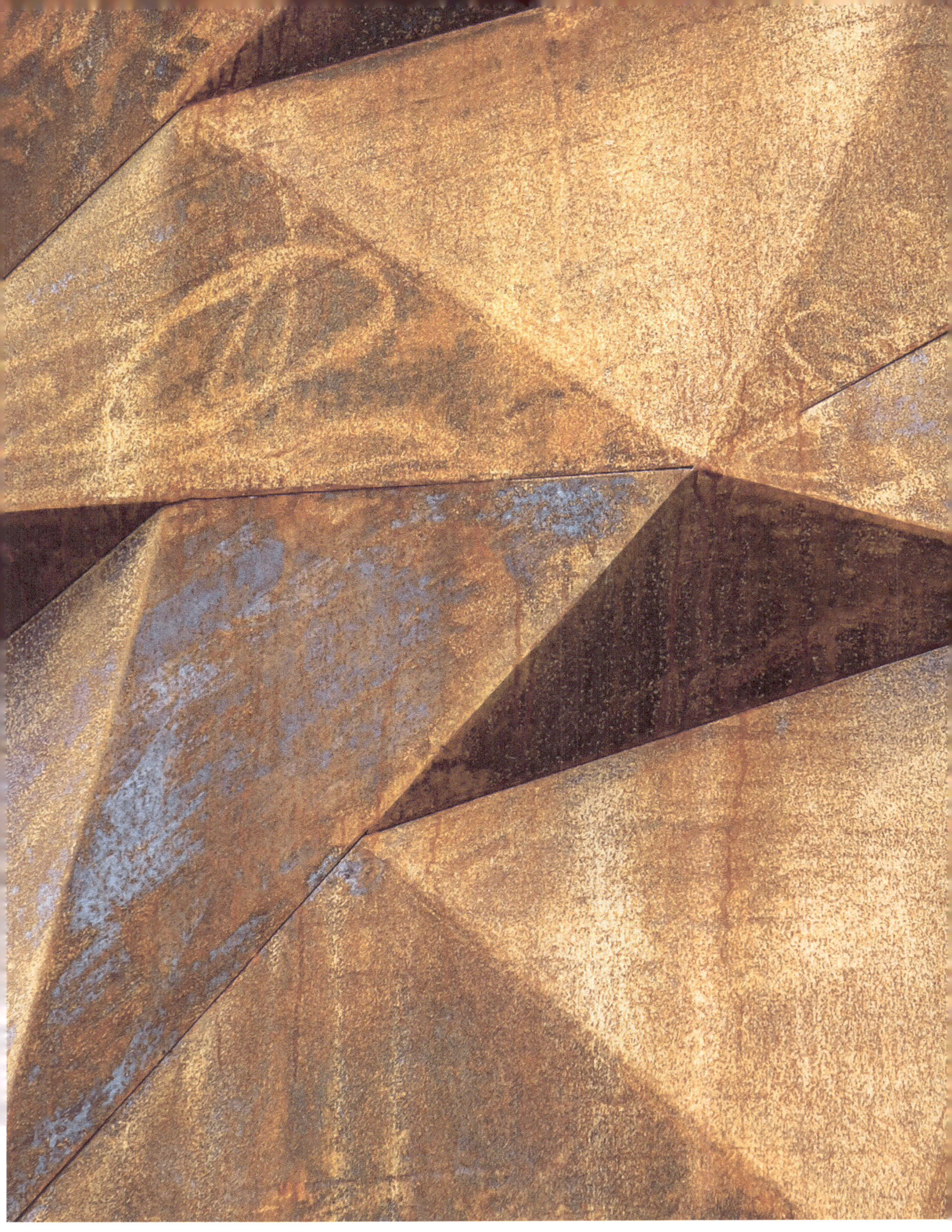

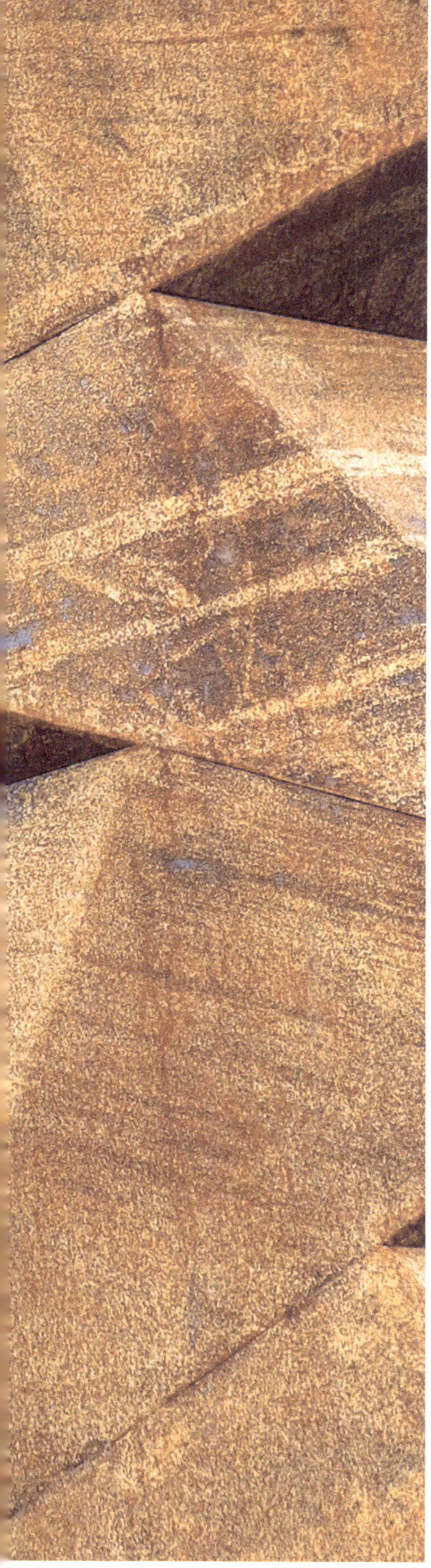

Scraper tool
Direction

Log in to the Cricut design space.
Create a new project.
Click on 'Upload Image.'
Drag the image to the design space.
Highlight the image and 'Flatten' it.
Click on the 'Make It' button.
Place vinyl on the cutting mat.
Custom dial the machine to vinyl.
Load the cutting mat into the machine.
Push the mat up against the rollers.
Cut the design out of the vinyl.
Weed out the excess vinyl with a weeding tool.
Apply a thin layer of transfer tape on the vinyl.
Peel off the backing.
Apply the transfer tape on the wall.
Smoothen with a scraper tool to let out the air bubbles.
Carefully peel off the transfer tape from the wall.

# WOODEN HAND-LETTERED SIGN

Materials and tools

Acrylic paint for whatever colors you would like
Vinyl
Cricut joy
Walnut hollow basswood planks
Transfer Tape
Scraper
An SVG file or font that you wish to use
Pencil
Eraser

Direction

You will need to start by deciding what you will want to draw onto the wood.

Then, place some lines on the plank to designate the horizontal and vertical axis for the grid. Set this aside for later.

Upload the file that you wish to use to the Design Space. Then, cut the file with the proper setting for vinyl.

Weed out the writing or design spaces that are not meant to go on the wood.

Using the transfer tape, apply the video to the top of the vinyl and smooth it out. Using the scraper and the transfer paper's corner, slowly peel the backing off a bit at a time. Do it carefully.

Remove the vinyl pieces' backing, aligning the lettering or design so that it is entirely centered. Place it carefully on the wooden plank.

Again, use the scraper to smooth out the vinyl on the plank.

Take off the transfer tape by smoothing off the bubbles as you scrape along with the wood sign. Discard the transfer tape at that time.

Continue to use the scraper to make the vinyl smoother. There should be no bumps since this creates bleeding.

Now, paint your wood plank with any color of your choice. Peel the vinyl letters off. Once the paint has completely dried, you can erase your pencil marks.

## COSMETIC BAG

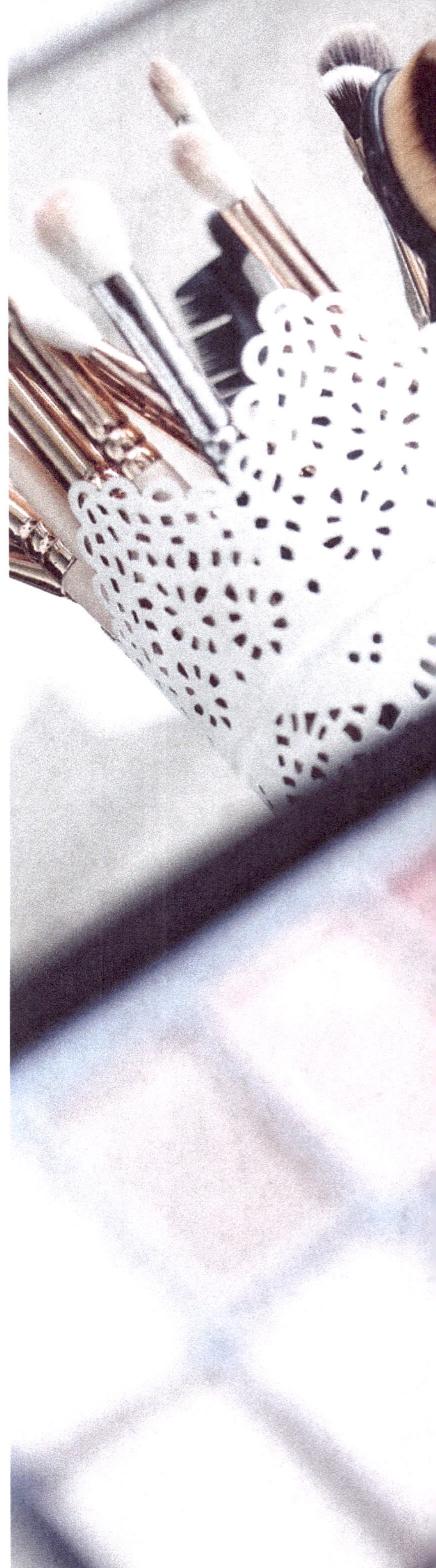

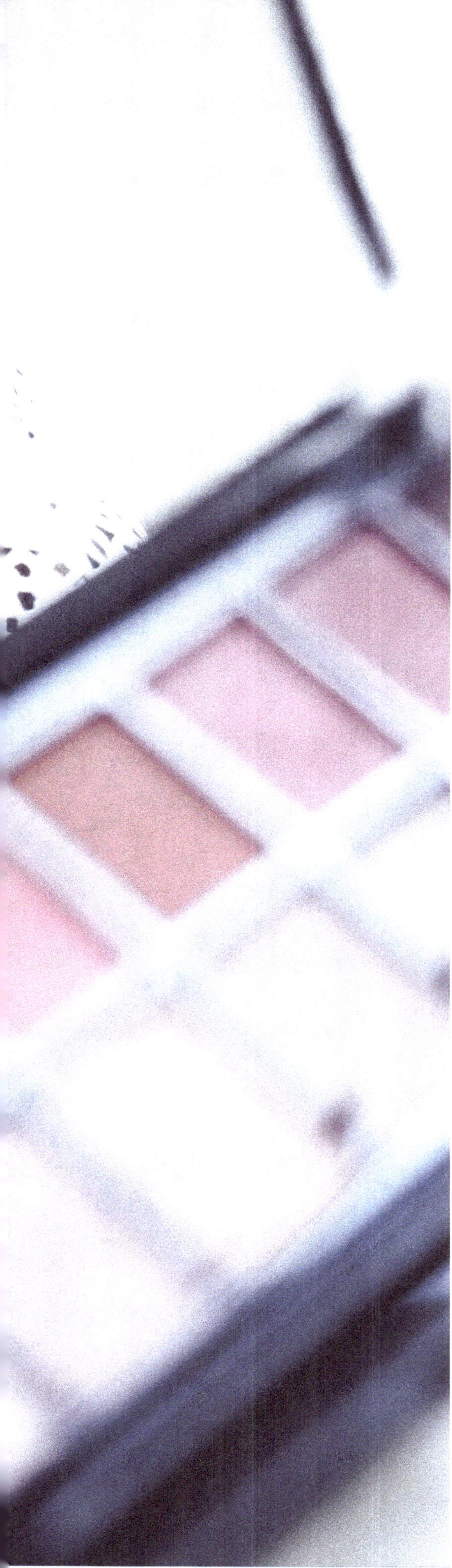

Materials and tools

Fabric for the outside
Thread
9-inch zipper
Lining fabric
Bags bottom fabric
Cosmetic bag pattern
Cricut
Cutting Mat

Direction

Open your pattern up anc cut out the pieces that you will need to make the cosmetic bag. While you are doing this, cut the lining that you will need also. Using the mat, cut the outer fabric and then the inner material. Use the 'Cotton' setting for the lining. Cut the bag's bottom with sturdy material and choose whichever setting matches the fabric used.

If you use the Cricut faux leather, you will have a sturdy bottom that does not cost as much as real leather but is just as sturdy.

Place the right sides together and sew one of the outside panels to the pieces used for the bottom. This should leave a 1/8-inch allowance for the seam. This should be the measurement for all seams.

Repeat this step with the lining and the bottom.

Next, place your zipper face down with the zipper's right side on the outside of the bag. Then, place the lining's top edge at the top of the zipper, lying face down. Line your edges pe-fectly and pin them together.

Using a zipper foot attachec to your sewing machine,

sew the zipper close to the teeth. At the end of the pull, stop and place the needle down into the material. Lift your sewing foot and pull your zipper from the machine past the point that is already sewed. Place the foot back down and continue sewing.

Iron this fabric so that it is smooth, and then sew a top stitch on the fabric's edge. Repeat this step on the other side.

Place the outside of the fabric lying face up, and then place the lining face down. Pin these pieces together with your zipper foot, following the same steps you did previously. Iron this side and then proceed to finish the topstitch.

Sew your other outside bottom piece and then sew the lining sides to the bottom of the lining. Make sure to leave the opening about a few inches wide so you can turn it inside out later on. Making sure you have the zipper open, proceed to sew the edges of the bag together. This should be the lining end to the bottom of your bag.

Proceed to sew the corners and then flatten the unseen edges and center your seams. Sew the piece closed and then repeat the process for the bottom as well as the lining.

Trim up all your hanging threads and the zipper parts that are sticking past the edge of your fabric bag. Using the unsewn hole flip the bag right side out and check your work.

Sew up your lining hole by folding the raw edge just a bit, making sure to sew close to the edge. Backstitch to make sure the sewing is permanent and trim the ends off.

Push your lining into the bag and push your

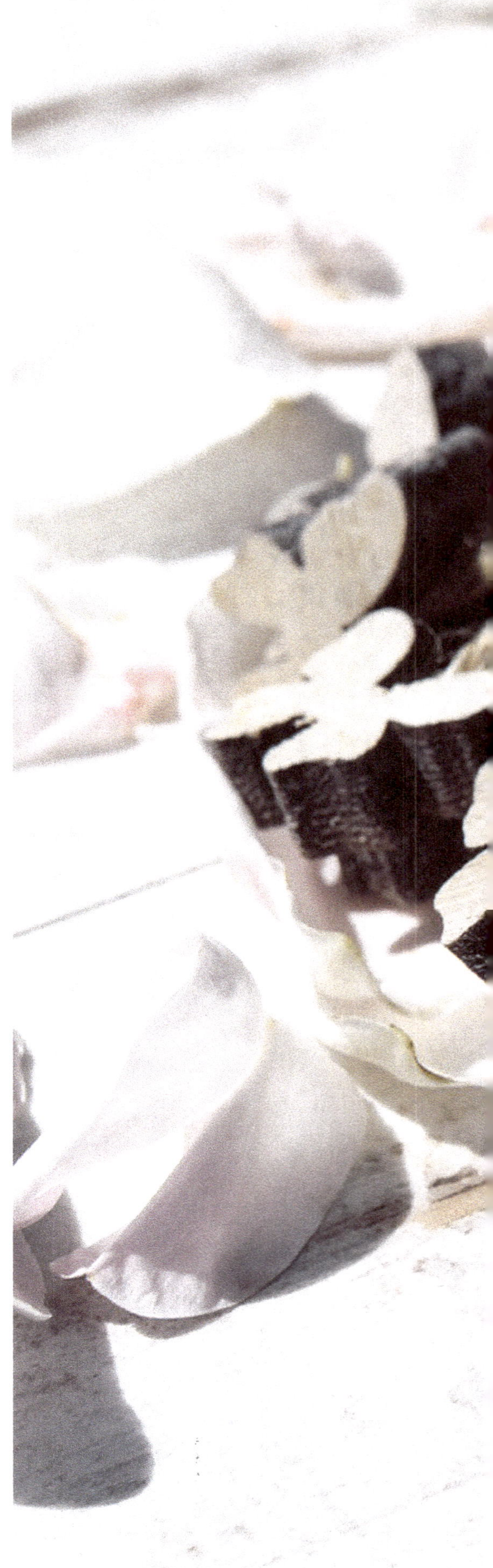

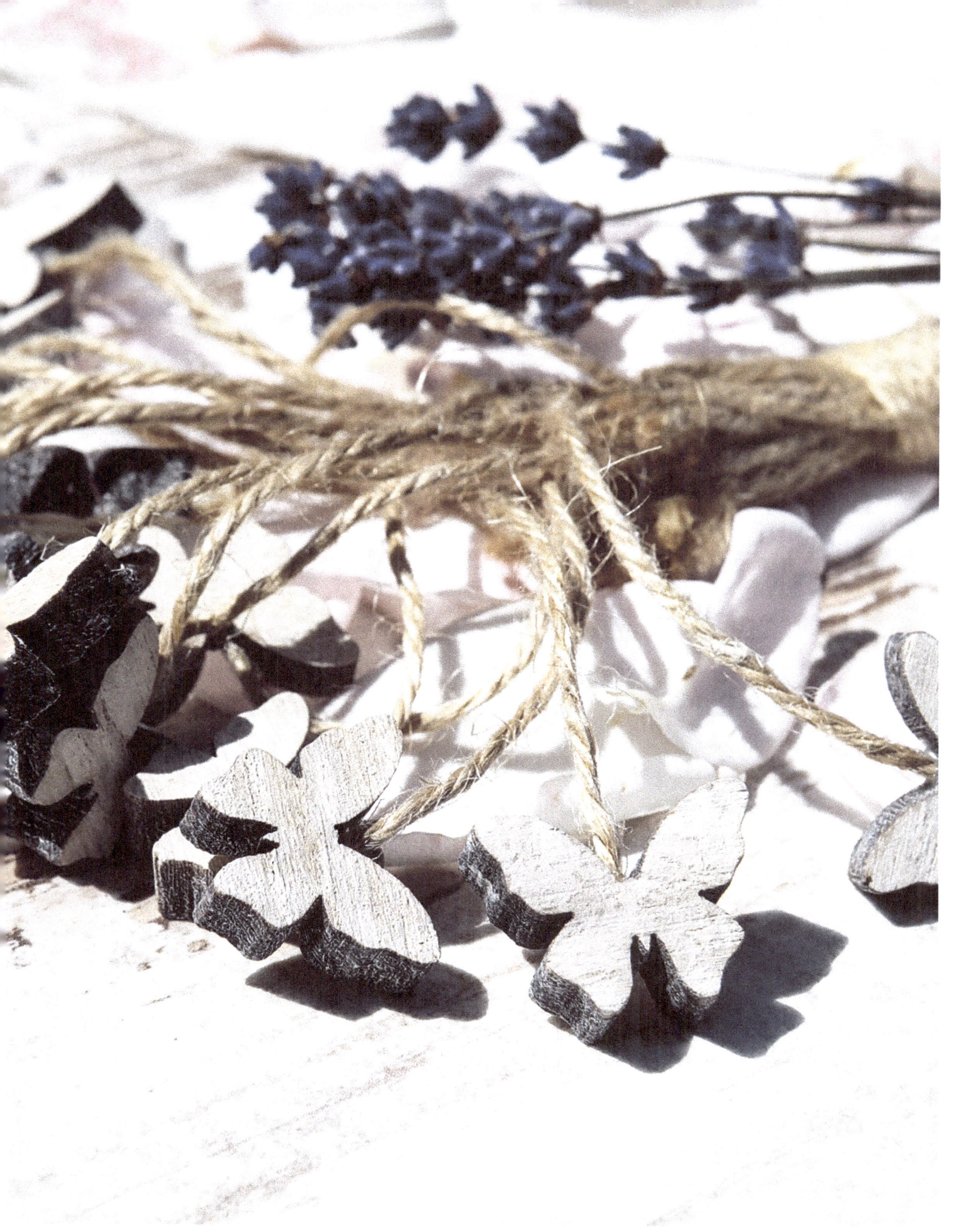

corners out of the bag to properly form the pack. Zip your zipper and admire your work.

# LEATHER GEOMETRIC BUFFALO PILLOW

Materials and tools

Cricut joy
Cricut X
Cardstock Cricut
Cutting Mat
Cricut Fine Point Blade Glue or Tape Runner

Direction

Use the connection above to resize the flowers to the size you need, then click 'Make It.'
Once cut, you can collect any parts you want. I hotly attached my toothpicks to the top of my cake. For the term topper, I used more giant wood skewers to stand above the flowers. Instead of flowers, this would be super sweet with mini paper rosettes.
Use paper and your Cricut joy to create custom cake decor. With every addition to the maker's tools, the Cricut joy has already made it so much easier to create the possibilities.

# FABRIC WREATH WITH FLOWERS
Materials and tools

A ring from an old lampshade
Ribbon to wrap the lampshade
Cricut joy

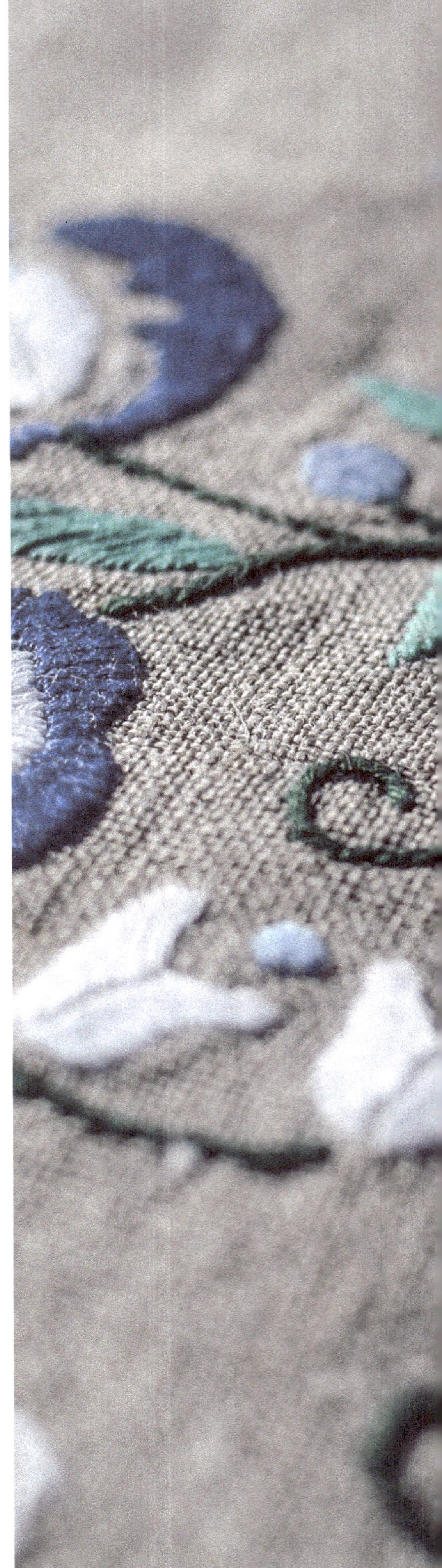

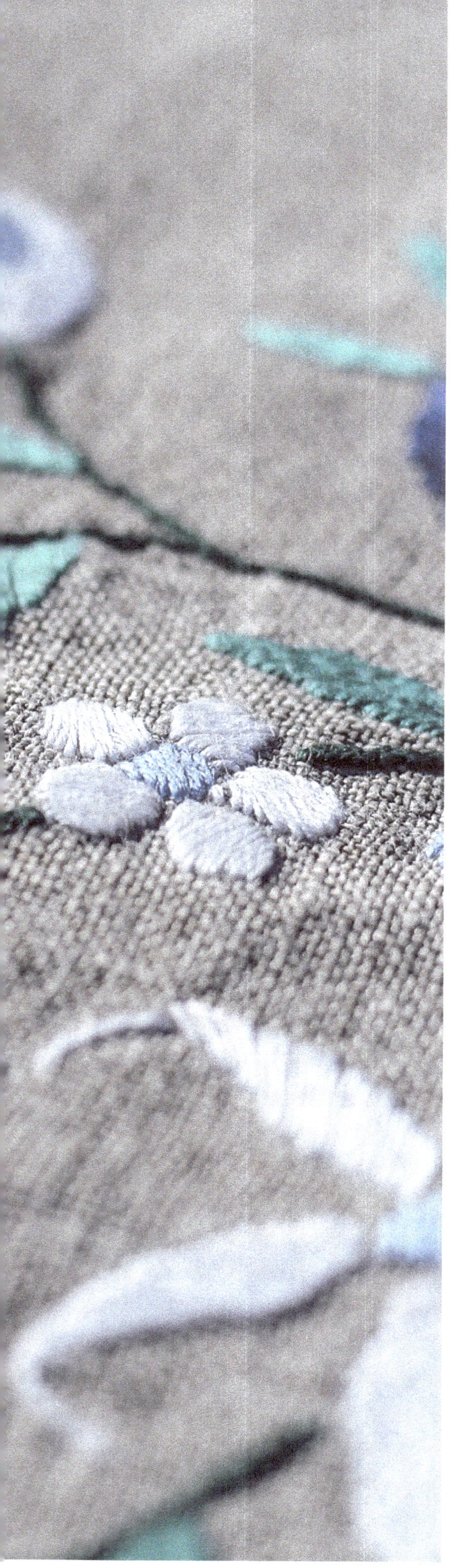

Cricut felt in various colors
Rotary blade
Cricut x mat for fabric
Hot glue gun and sticks of glue
Felt balls
Wreath forms

Direction

Using your Cricut Design Space, you need to log in.
In the Cricut Design Space, you will need to click on 'New Project' and then select the image that you would like to use for your flowers. You can use the search bar on the right-hand side at the top to locate the idea that you wish to use.
Next, click on the image and click 'Insert Image' so that the image is selected.
Click on each of the files in the image file. Click the button that says 'Flatten' at the lower right section of the screen. This will turn the individual pieces into one whole piece. This prevents the cut file from being unique pieces for the image.
Now, you want to resize the image so that it is the size you wish it to be. This can be any size that is within the recommended space for the size of the canvas.
If you want duplicates of the image for a sheet of flowers, you should 'Select All' and then edit the image and click 'Copy.' This will allow you to copy the whole row you selected. Once you have copied, you can then edit and paste the multiple images to make a sheet. This is the easiest way to copy and paste the image over and over again. Using the project that is listed in the Cricut ma-

nual, you can find the directions for the flowers. Once the flowers are cut out, you can begin to place them together with the listed instructions below.

Using each one of the succulents, place the tabs together using the glue. Secure your leaves together. Repeat each piece until they are done. Stack them together to create a succulent. Use the hot glue and place the smaller circle in the center of the finished ones. Each flower should be stacked three pieces tall with a small dot in the center.

After the flowers and the succulents are assembled, you can begin to arrange them all over the ring covered in ribbon. Using the glue, place the flowers in the order that you want to cover the call or in a decorative fashion.

# SUGAR SKULLS WITH THE CRICUT

Materials and tools

Printer
Toothpicks
Standard cardstock
x standard grip mat for Cricut
Sugar skull 'Print then Cut' image
Cricut Explore machine
Cricut Design space software
Glue

Direction

Using your Cricut Design Space, you need to log in.

In the Cricut Design Space, you will need to click

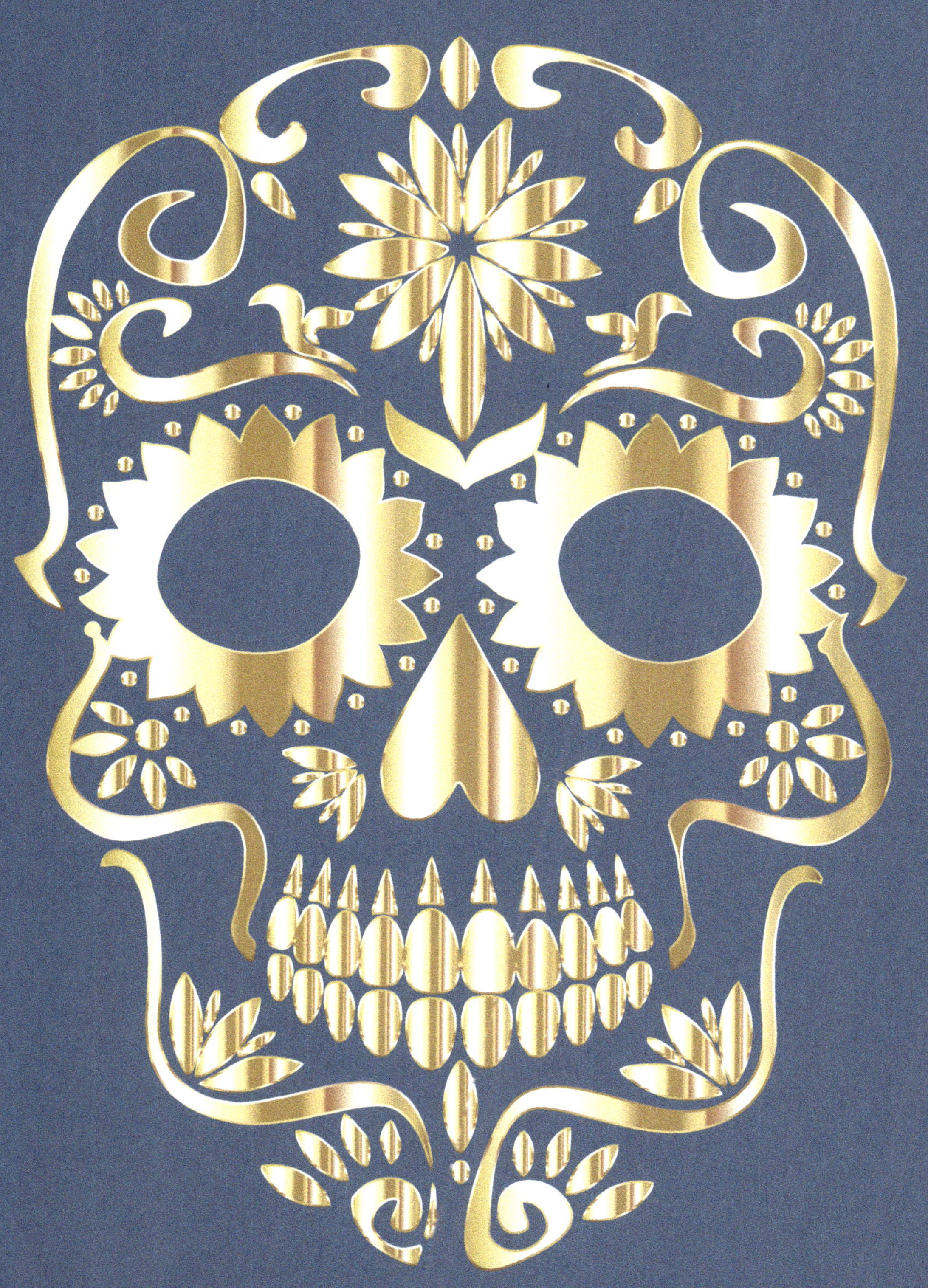

on 'New Project' and then select the image you would like to use for your sugar skulls. You can use the search bar on the right-hand side at the top to locate the image that you wish to use.

Next, click on the image and click 'Insert Image' to select the image.

Click on each file in the image and click the button that says 'Flatten' at the lower right section of the screen. This will turn the individual pieces into one whole piece. This prevents the cut file from being unique pieces for the image.

Now, you want to resize the image so that it is the size you wish it to be. This can be any size that is within the recommended space for the size of the canvas.

If you want duplicates of the image for the sheet of sugar skulls, you should 'Select All' and then edit the image and click 'Copy.' This will allow you to copy the whole row you selected. Once you have copied, you can then edit and paste the multiple images to make a sheet. This is the easiest way to copy and paste the image over and over again.

Follow the instructions that are on the screen for printing, then cut the sugar skull images.

Using glue, piece the front and back of the sugar skull together to create the topper with the toothpick inserted into the pieces' center.

## PENDANT WITH MONOGRAM

Materials and tools
Necklace chain
Jewelry pliers
Cricut gold pen
Cricut Explore Air
Cricut strong mat grip

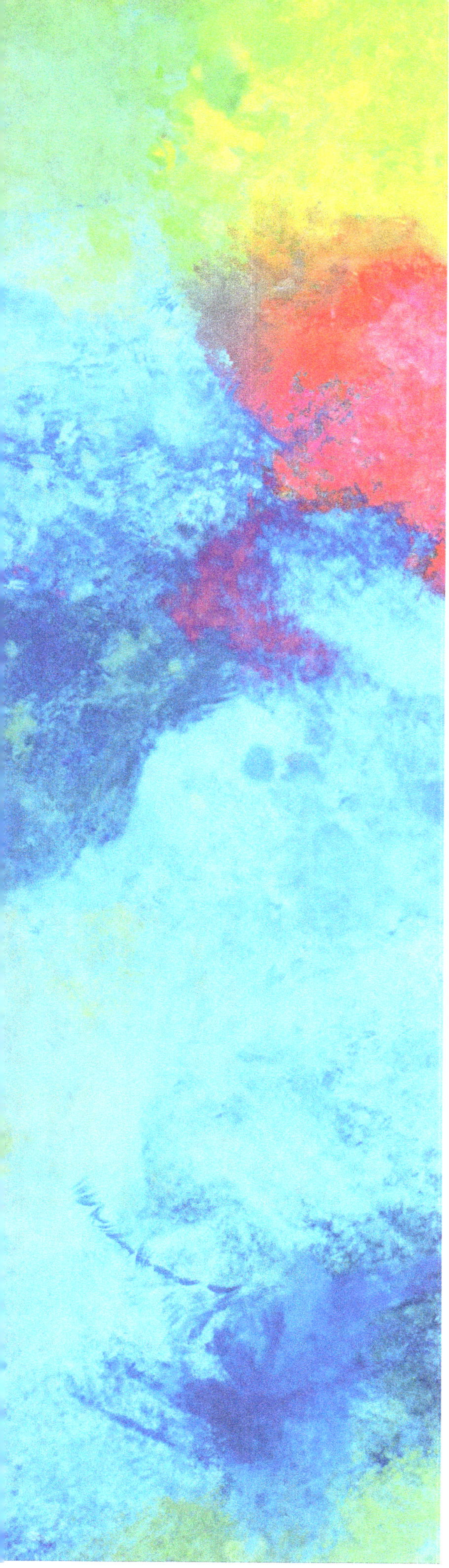

Cricut Faux leather
Jump ring
Fabric fusion

Direction

Start by opening the Cricut Design Space. Choose the size that you want the pendant to be. This can be a circle pendant. Using the machine, make another circular-sized pendant.
Attach the jump ring here later after the circles have been made.
Next, open the text section in the Design shop, and type in the exact initials you would like to use.
Select the section with a 'writing style' option from the menu and adjust the font of the lettering to whatever you wish.
Drag your letter to the center part of the circle and resize it to fit the appropriate size.
Be sure to make a front and a back. This will ensure both sides of the piece look like leather.
Create your circle so that it matches the other one minus the letter.
Make this an attached set.
Using the Cricut pen, begin to cut the pieces. As it is missing the leather, it will print the initials.
Use your fabric fusion glue to join the two pieces of leather together, making the pendant.
Using the pliers for jewelry, you can twist on the ring for the necklace.
Attach your pendant and jump ring, and then string it onto the chain.
The pliers can close the jump ring off.

# Chapter 5
# Cricut Joy FAQ

## WHY DOES DESIGN SPACE SAY MY CRICUT MACHINE IS ALREADY IN USE WHEN IT□S NOT?

To resolve this, make sure that you've completed the New Machine Setup for your Cricut. Try Design Space in another browser. The two that work best are Google Chrome and Mozilla Firefox; if it doesn't work in one of those, try the other. If that doesn't clear the error, try a different USB port and USB cable. Disconnect the machine from the computer and turn it off. While it's off, restart your computer. After your computer restarts, re-connect the device and turn it on. Wait a few moments, and then try Design Space again. If you're still having the same problem, contact Cricut Member Care.

## WHY DOESN□T MY CUT MATCH THE PREVIEW IN DESIGN SPACE?

Test another image and see if the same thing happens. If it's only happening with one

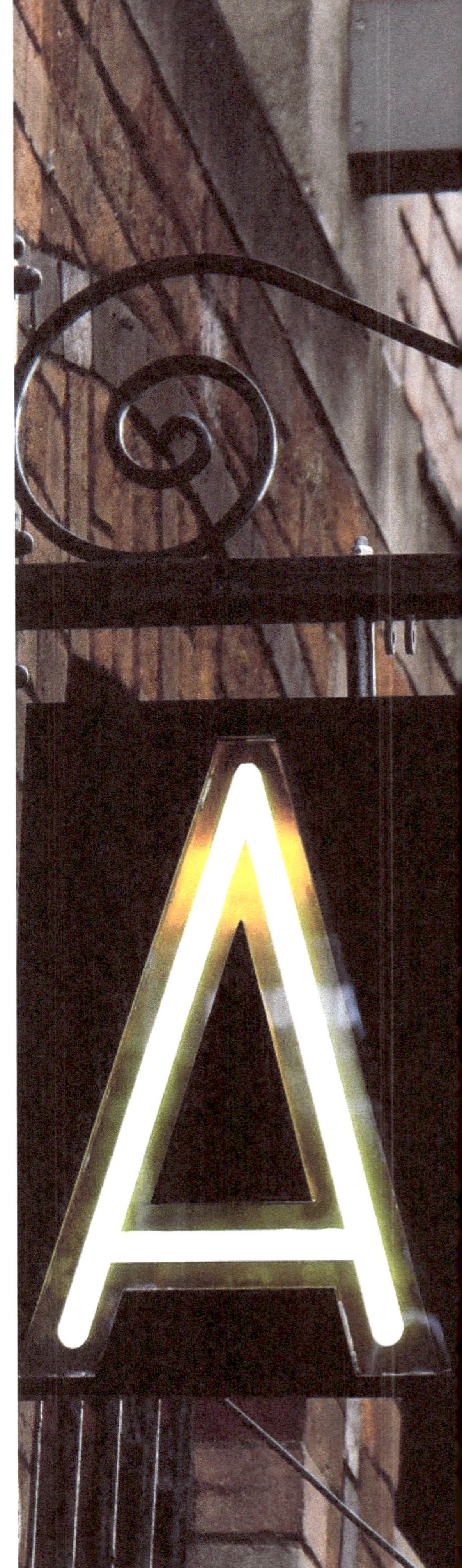

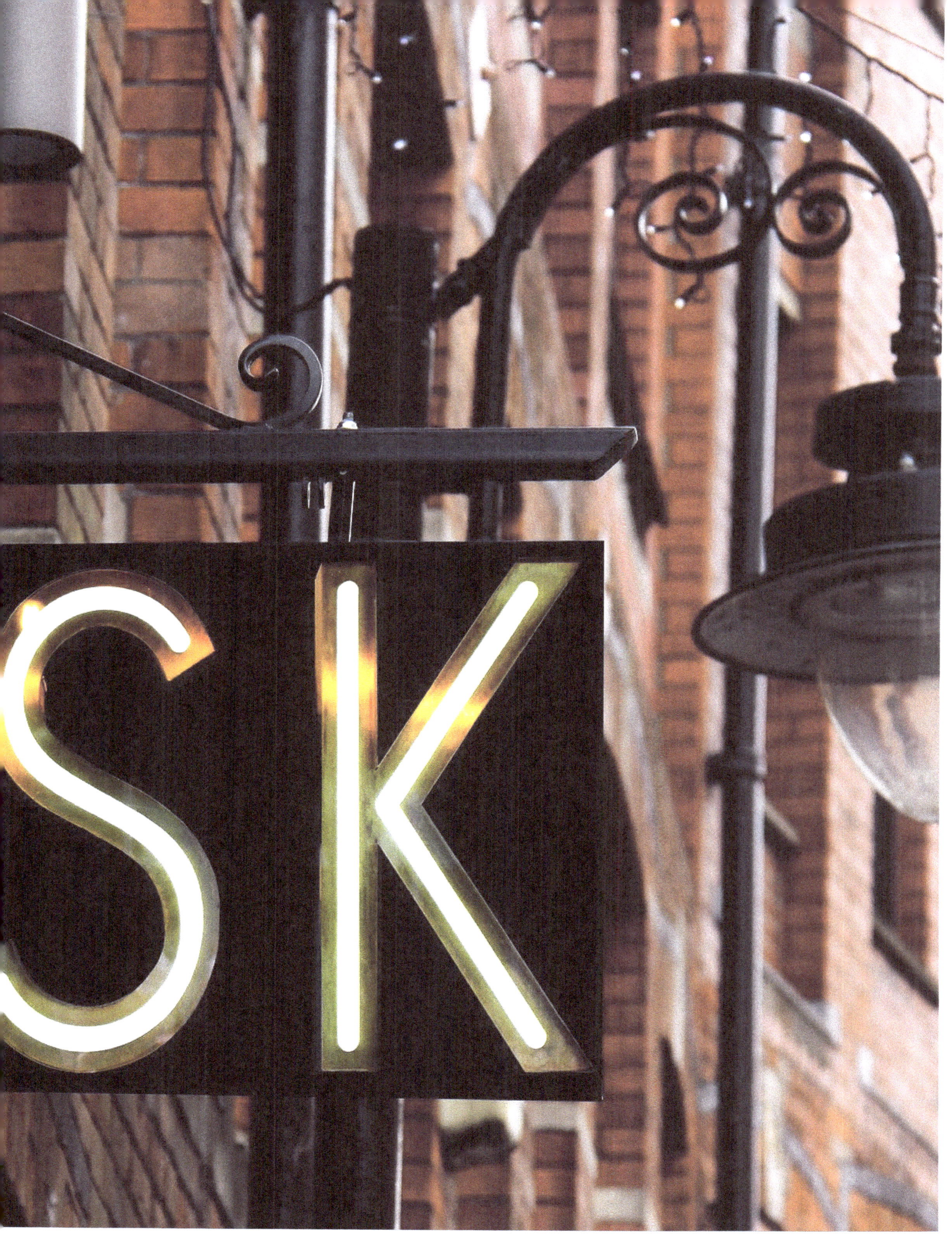
SK

project, create a new project and start over or try a different image. If it happens with a second project, and your machine is connected with Bluetooth, disconnect that and plug it in with a USB cable. Larger projects may sometimes have difficulty communicating the cuts over Bluetooth. If you can't connect with USB or the problem is still occurring, check that your computer matches or exceeds the running Design Space system requirements. If it doesn't, try the project on a different computer or mobile device that does. Suppose your computer does meet the criteria, open Design Space in a different browser, and try again. If the problem continues, try a different USB cable. Finally, if the issue still hasn't been resolved, contact Cricut Member Care.

## WHAT DO I DO IF I NEED TO INSTALL USB DRIVERS FOR MY CRICUT MACHINE?

Typically, the Cricut drivers are automatically installed when you connect them with a USB cable. If Design Space doesn't see your machine, you can try this to troubleshoot the driver installation. First, open Device Manager on your computer. You'll need to have administrator rights. For Windows 7, click Start, right-click on Computer, and select Manage.

## WHY DOES MY CRICUT JOY SAY THE BLADE IS NOT DETECTED?

Ensure that the tool in Clamp B is the same one Design Space recommends in the Load Tools step


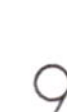

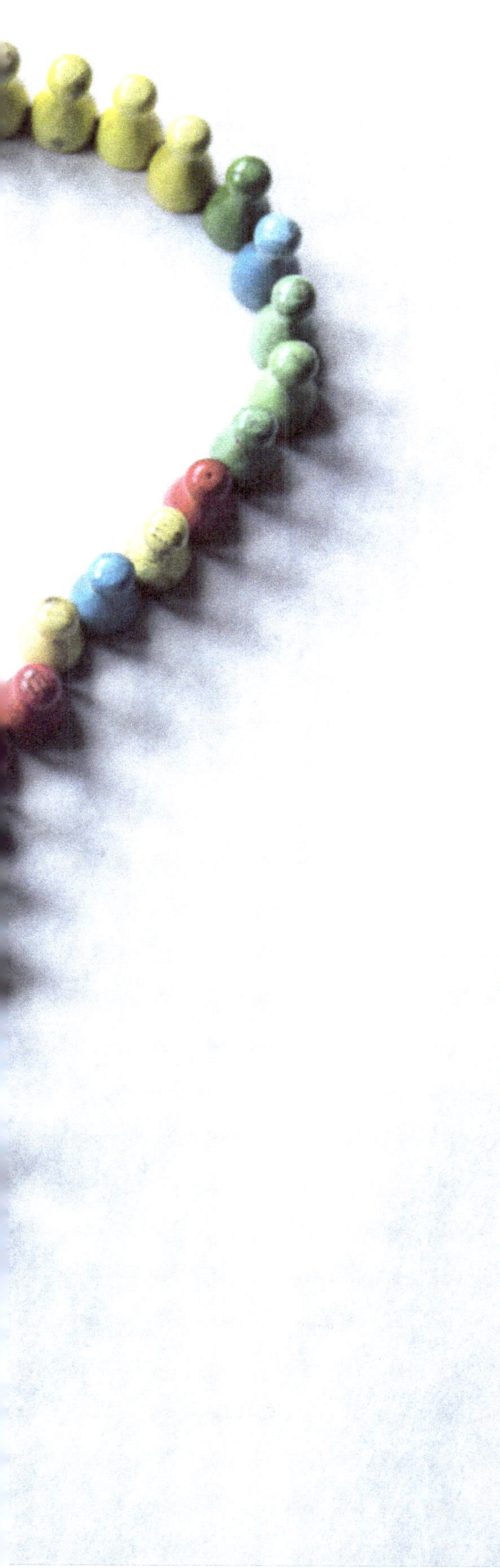

of the Project Preview screen. If you don't have that recommended tool, unload your mat and select Edit Tools on the Project Preview screen. Here, you can choose a different device. If the machine and the selection already march, carefully remove Clamp B's tool and clean the housing's reflective band. Reinstall it in the clamp and press the Go button. If that doesn't resolve the problem, remove the tool again and clean the machine's sensor. Reinstall the device and press Go again.

## WHY IS MY CRICUT MACHINE MAKING A GRINDING NOISE?

If it's the carriage car making a loud noise after you press the cut button, and it sounds like the carriage might be hitting the side of the machine, record a short video of it and send it to Cricut Member Care. If the noise comes from a brand-new device the first time you use it, contact Cricut Member Care. Otherwise, make sure that you're using the original power cord that came with your machine. If the machine isn't getting the correct voltage, it may produce a grinding sound. If you are using the machine's power cord, adjust your pressure settings. If it's too high, it might produce an unusual sound. Decrease it in increments of 2-4 and do some test cuts. If it's still making the issue even after decreasing the cutting pressure, contact Cricut Member Care.

## WHY IS MY MAT GOING INTO THE MACHINE CRO-OKED?

Check the roller bar to see if it's loose, damaged, or uneven. If it is, take a photo or video of it to send to Cricut Member Care. If the roller bar seems fine, make sure that you're using the right mat size for the machine. Make sure the mat is correctly lined up with the guides and that the edge is underneath the roller bar when you prepare to load it. If it's still loading crookedly even when properly lined up with the guides, try applying gentle pressure to the mat to get it under the roller bar once it starts. If none of this works, contact Cricut Member Care.

## WHAT DO I DO IF MY CRICUT JOY STOPPED PARTWAY THROUGH A CUT?

If the Knife Blade stops cutting and the Go button is flashing, the Maker has encountered some error. In Design Space, you'll get a notification that the blade is stuck. This might have been caused by the edge running into something like a knot or seam if too much dust or debris built up in the cut area or if the blade got into a gouge in the mat from a previous cut. To resume your project, do not unload the mat. This will lose your place in the project, and it will be impossible to get it lined up again. Check the cut area for dust or debris, and gently clean it.

Why is my fabric getting caught under the rollers? Be sure to cut down any fabric so that it fits on your mat without going past the adhesive. If you have stuck the material and realize it's hanging past the adhesive, use a ruler and a sharp blade to trim it. Or, if it's the correct size but slightly

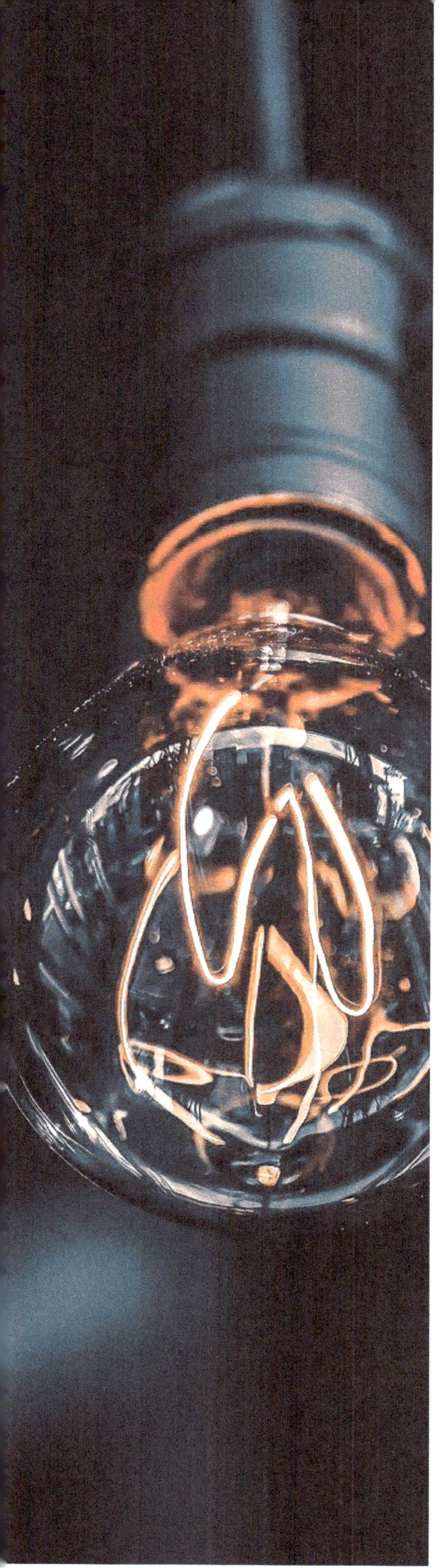

askew, unstick it and reposition it.

## DO THE DESIGN SPACE OF THE CRICUT JOY AND THAT OF EXPLORE DIFFER?

No, Circuit joy's design space is similar to that of the Cricut Explore, with its URL location being similar (design.cricut.com) and can be accessed through the same Cricut Identity via a sign-in. However, the Cricut joy lacks a smart Set dial, meaning that once you select the cut operation, the Cricut joy selects the materials and loads the machine's tools.

## DOES THE CRICUT JOY CUT FABRIC PATTERNS SUCH AS CLOTHES, PANTS, SHIRTS, SKIRTS, BLOUSES, ETC.?

Absolutely Yes, the Cricut Machine can cut through fabric patterns. The Cricut joy comes with 25 patterns for sewing to assist you in getting started. Also, the Cricut joy comes with hundreds of design patterns in collaboration with Simplicity.

## DOES THE CRICUT JOY ETCH THROUGH GLASS?

Yes, the Cricut joy can etch glass but not directly. To do this, you need to create and cut your design patterns using the Design space and applying an etching cream onto the glass surface.

Do I lose my projects, uploaded images, and cartridges when upgrading the Cricut Maker?

No. Your projects, cartridges, and uploaded images remain intact, the reason being that you typically use a Cricut ID in the Cricut cloud and not machines with the same Cricut ID and not the machine itself. So, you can be sure all your content will be accessible with the Cricut Maker.

## DOES THE CRICUT JOY ENGRAVE METALLIC MATERIALS SUCH AS JEWELRY OR PET ID TAGS?

Yes, but to technically achieve this, you need a unique etching tool for it to go through a third party. This is because the deep engraving functionality may fail on some metallic objects. You may need an etching tool by "Choma's creation," which fits into the Cricut joy other devices. With the tool, you can engrave or etch material such as leather, metal clay, silver, aluminum, bronze, copper, plastic, and acrylic

## DO I NEED A PRINTER? WHAT PRINTER SHOULD I USE?
## ABSOLUTELY

No, Cricut machines are not dependent upon printers.
As far as what printer to get, you just need something that prints color! One of the most versatile Hp machines is the HP Envy, but there are many great printers out there in the market that are not limited to Hp.

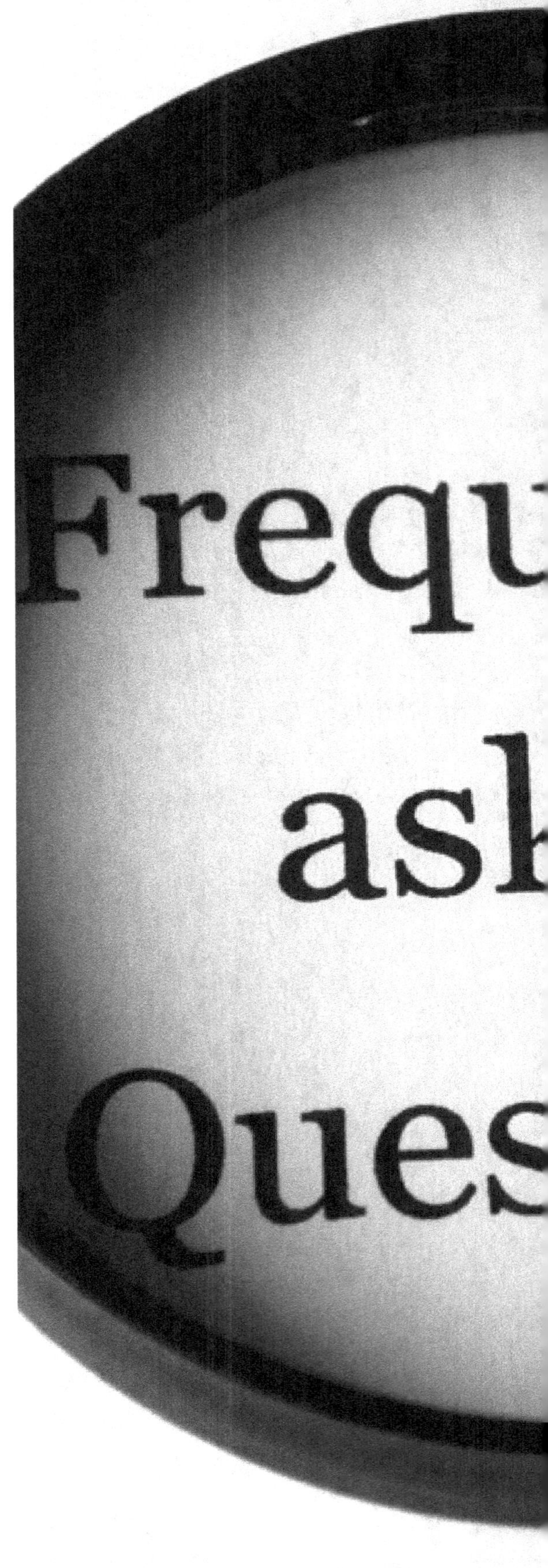

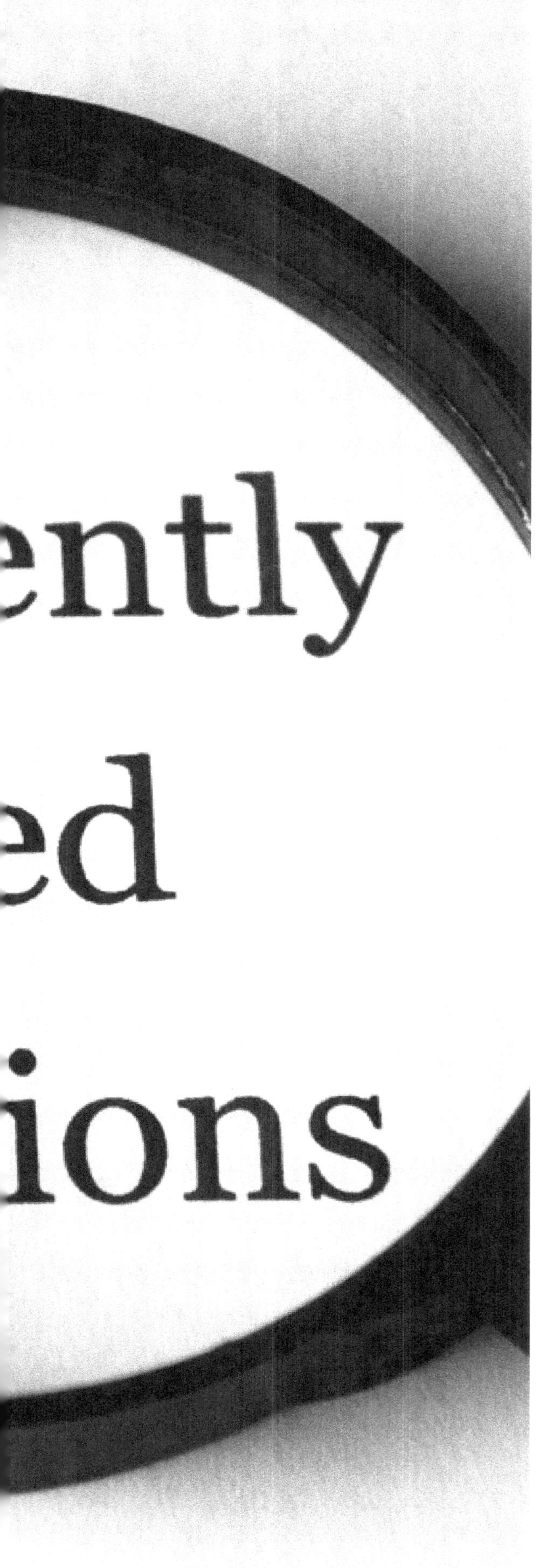


### DOES THERE EXIST ANY DIFFERENCE IN THE POWER CORDS OF THE CRICUT MACHINE?

No, there is a physical difference in the Power cords of the Cricut Machines. However, there is a difference in the output current with the Cricut Maker's cable upgraded to supply 3A with its predecessors-Cricut Explore having a 2.5A output current supply. This adaption also allows you to charge your mobile phone via its charging port on the right-hand side while multitasking the cutting/writing functionalities.

However, if you were using Cricut Explore, you can still charge the mobile phone device. Still, the difference is that because of its low current capacity, it will either slow, stutter, or even shut off (in extreme cases: because the device will need a current supply in addition to the cutting operation -which needs more current supply especially as it requires more cutting pressure.

What materials can I cut using the Cricut Maker? The Cricut engineering team is in the process of experimenting with more materials, cutting pressures, and guidelines. However, the following are some of the materials it cuts; fabric, papers-crepe and tissue, vinyl, cardstock, cork, leather, duct tape, faux leather, chipboard, felt, adhesive foil, among others.

### HOW DOES THE ROTARY CUTTER DIFFER FROM THE FABRIC BLADE?

The Cricut Maker can use both the rotary blade and the bonded fabric blade. However, the difference is that the rotary cutter can cut through delicate materials without backing material. In contrast, the rotary blade will need to use the Adaptive tool system to perform the precision cutting experience. What is the Pink Mat, and how can I use it?

The Pink Mat is useful for cutting fabrics as well as other delicate materials. It is highly durable therefore vital, which means it can withstand pressure when cutting thin materials. You may be asking how it needs a strong material, whereas the material undercut is narrow. It takes a lot of stress when cutting delicate fabrics, meaning it needs to stay flat on the mat to resist the need to shift.

What do I get once I purchase the Cricut Maker? Once you purchase the Cricut joy, you will get the following: warranty information, Fine point black pen, USB cord, power cord, sample materials, rotary blade, fine-tip blade, two mats.

## ARE BLADES AND TOOLS OF THE CRICUT JOY AND OTHER PREDECESSORS INTERCHANGEABLE?

Yes and No. The Cricut joy cannot be used in the Cricut Explore machines; however, the Cricut Explore machines can use Cricut joy's blades. Only the reason being the Cricut joy came after the Cricut Explore; therefore, the functionalities of the Cricut Explore differ from that the Circuit joy, with the latter being more advanced compared to the Explore. It does not have the drive gears that control the rotary blade and knife, for starters, and the pressure required to operate these tools are not present in the Explore.

Does the Cricut joy have a Fast mode configuration? The machine has a fast mode alternative for writing



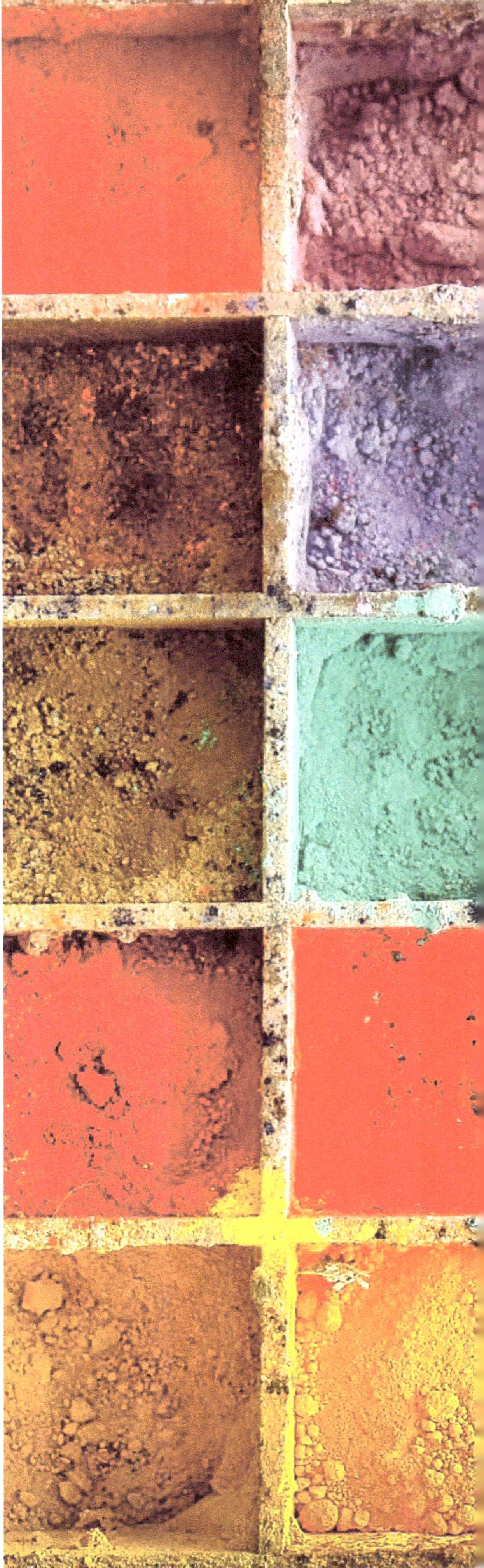

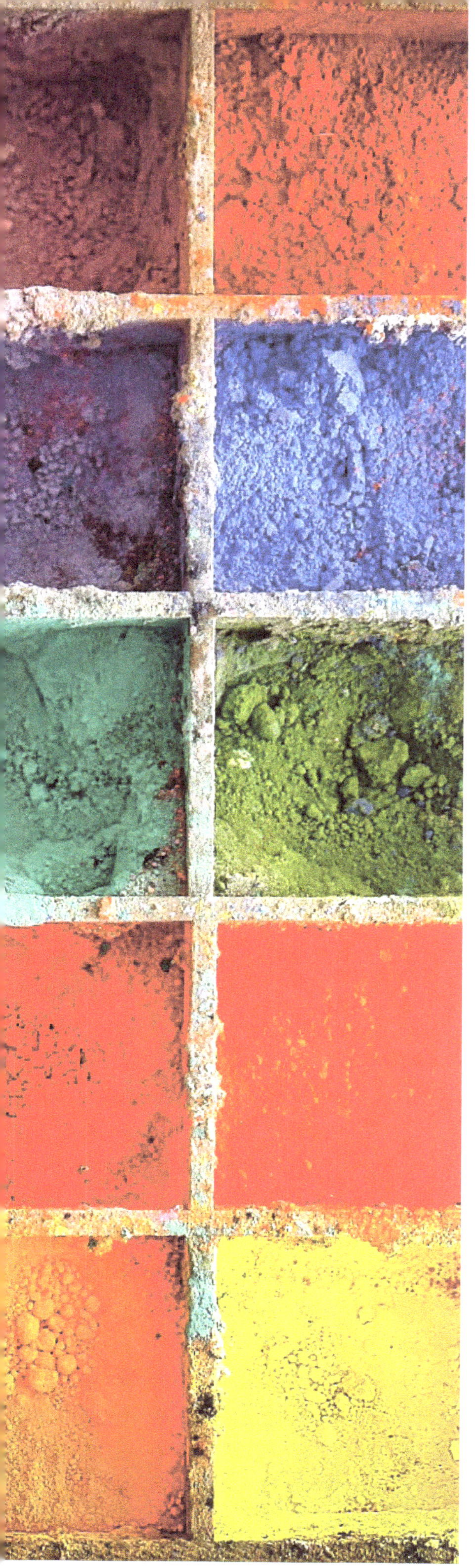

and cutting up to two times faster, especially when using the Cardstock, Iron-on, and Vinyl settings.

## HOW DOES THE CRICUT JOY DIFFER FROM ITS PRE-DECESSORS IN TERMS OF SOFTWARE?

Both are similar in terms of software because they use the Cricut Design Space. This means that all the Explore projects can be cut by the Cricut joy, whereas some Cricut joy project can also be missed by the Cricut Explore as long as it does not concern the rotary and knife blades.

## HOW CAN I KNOW IF THE CRICUT JOY KNOWS THAT A BLADE HAS BEEN LOADED?

When you select the cut operation, the machine will first move the carriage to the right side, and it will scan the blade to discover which one has been installed in the Cricut Maker.

## WHAT IS THE MAXIMUM THICKNESS SPECIFICATION FOR MY CUTTING MATERIALS WHEN WORKING WITH CRICUT MAKER?

The maximum allowed thickness of the Cricut joy is 2.4mm or 3/32" inches for both the knife and rotary blades.

## DOES THIS MACHINE NEED AN INTERNET CON-NECTION?

Absolutely yes, The Cricut joy machine is used with

Design Space, a cloud-based, online software. It does not function stand-alone. When using Design Space on a desktop or laptop computer, an internet connection is required.

## HOW CAN I USE THE CRICUT JOY WHERE I LACK ACCESS TO A COMPUTER?

Unfortunately, if you lack access to a computer, the only option you have is to use an IPad to access the design space. Other Android-based tablets are not compatible with the design space.

## WHERE CAN ONE OBTAIN IMAGES FOR CRICUT PROJECTS?

With the internet, there are lots of sites you can obtain images for making that Cricut Project success for free. However, if you may need to get high-quality images to complete that project a tremendous success, you can consider the following paid image sites; Etsy, Craft Bundles, So Fontsy. Additionally, you can pay the Cricut Access subscription fee to access many images and fonts from Cricut's images library.

## WHERE CAN I PURCHASE THE CRICUT JOY MACHINE?

The Cricut joy machine can easily be purchased locally from available shops and trusted dealers of Cricut Supplies, but here are some of the favorite online websites you can get the Cricut Maker; the official website-Cricut Online store, Amazon, and Michaels.

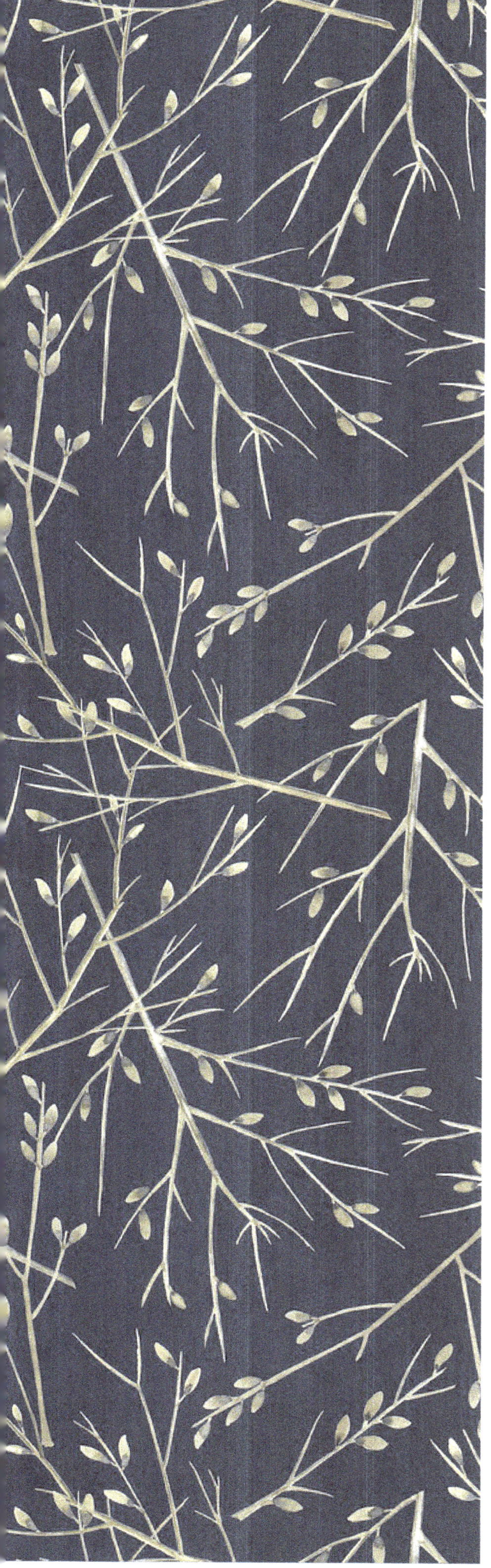

## WHICH ARE SOME OF THE BEST PLACES TO PURCHASE APPAREL FOR THE CRICUT MAKER?

Cricut is popularly known for its apparel projects as it can be rather expensive to purchase bags and t-shirts regularly. You can typically obtain plain T-shirts from online stores and shops for as little as $3.

## WHAT ACCESSORIES DO I NEED FOR MY CRICUT MAKER?

There are a lot of accessories available - and let us be real. You do not need all of them! You can also find more information online using the following keywords: - Essential Cricut Accessories for Beginners

## WHERE CAN I GET THE ADDITIONAL SUPPORT OF THE CRICUT MAKER?

With the rise of technology, you can quickly get information concerning absolutely anything on the Cricut joy from the internet. One of the websites you can quickly obtain more information is the Cricut website (www.cricut.com). Additionally, you may use the website and other related websites to get more inspiration for the Cricut Maker projects.

# Conclusion

When you choose the machine that will work best with you, you will find that the company's website is much cheaper than the other retailers that you can find online. The benefit of buying from the company itself is that you do not have to deal with a third party. Instead, you get coupons, bundles, and discounts that you are looking for, and there is no problem with the machine. In addition to that, when you buy from a third-party retailer, they do not let you bundle at all, so you will be paying an extra per item you want. This can get very expensive very quickly. First, set out to be different. Simply act naturally. Carry your idiosyncrasy and inventiveness to the table. Please keep it simple and narrow. Do not intend to be the Walmart of the specialty world; mean to be a specialist and the best there is in your general vicinity of slyness. So, pause for a moment and choose what you will know for.

Be consistent. Work on your Cricut business reliably. In an ideal world, you should work consistently. Some of you may simply need to sell as a diversion and can take a shot at it once every week. Whatever your calendar is, do it as reliably as could reasonably be expected. You're never going to go anyplace if you overlook your business for quite a long time or months one after another. Be reliable with estimating and quality as well. Your clients should realize what's in store for you. They will recommend you to others again and again if they know they can rely on you.

In this book, we have given you the tools to make your Cricut work at its best all day, every day. When you can do this, you will be able to make anything that you want because these machines can cut amazingly well, and they have so many functions that they could make your head spin. This book has been able to help you see the difference between the different machines and how and why the prices are different. Each device has something that it does best, and the Maker is the best of the four as it can cut more than any other machine. This means that you get to work with new materials that you will not use with the other devices because they can't cut them. They call the Maker the ultimate machine because it can do what others can't.

Our journey within the colorful world of Cricut Joy has come to an end. But your learning journey never stops. Continue to get excited about colors and shapes, make small objects that will help you in your everyday life, and never stop being curious.

I, Sienna Tally, will continue to accompany you with more adventures and practical, simple guides into the world of Cricut. For more information, please see my bibliography.

Happy crafting, thank you!

Thank

you !!

www.ingramcontent.com/pod-product-compliance
Lightning Source LLC
Chambersburg PA
CBHW080456030726
47592CB00011B/3140